For everyone who cooks!

Special thanks to all who contributed ideas and encouragement, tested recipes, or tried a recipe and let us know they loved it or how to make it better. A curtsy to the great cooks who taught us so much: Julia Child, Marcella Hazan, Edna Lewis, Deborah Madison, Jacques Pépin. Appreciation to Elizabeth Hanna, doctoral student at Rutgers University and Registered Dietician Nutritionist, for her review of recipes. Extra special thanks to Jason, our foodies-in-training—Rocky, Orion and Max—Michael A. Giaquinto, Lucy Loomis, Ellen Adamson and all our mothers and grandmothers, who led the way.

We are proud to pledge a percentage of our book sales to support organizations that provide hunger relief and nutritional education.

Distribution by KDP Amazon and Ingram Spark (P.O.D.)
Printed in the United States of America and Canada

Title: The $5 Foodie
Names: Lucy Holland, Carol Rizzoli, Ethan Eron, Amanda Eron, and Hugo Rizzoli (authors)
Website: https://www.thefivedollarfoodie.com/

Title page: Carol Rizzoli with bounty from Cape Cod Organic Farm
Back cover: Liliya Kandrashevich/Shuttershock (left), Five Dollar Foodies (center), and Anna Shepulova/Shuttershock (right)
Image credits: Lucy Loomis (page 44), Anna Shepulova/Shutterstock (pages 47 and 58), Vania Georgieva/Shutterstock (page 76), ChameleonsEye/Shutterstock (page 80), Liliya Kandrashevich/Shutterstock (page 82), Elena Veselova/Shutterstock (page 112), Anna Pustynnikova/Shutterstock (pages 117 and 125), Bluebird Provisions/Pexels (page 129), Rimma Bondarenko/Shutterstock (page 130).

Paperback ISBN: 979-8-9850864-1-6
Hardcover ISBN: 979-8-9850864-2-3
E-book ISBN: 979-8-9850864-0-9

Book description: Not your typical budget cookbook, the $5 Foodie shows you that a no-frills grocery bill doesn't have to come at the expense of your health, your tastebuds, or your environmental footprint.

THE $5 FOODIE

Cook Better, Spend Less, Enjoy More

Lucy Holland and Carol Rizzoli

with Ethan Eron, Amanda Eron and Hugo Rizzoli

Food costs are provided as estimates and will fluctuate depending on where you shop, what is on sale or abundant in season, and they may increase or decrease with market conditions.
For up-to-the-minute pricing, see thefivedollarfoodie.com.

CONTENTS

INTRODUCTION

When we cook, we want fantastic flavor, comfort one day and bursts of world spice the next. We want it healthful, quick and inexpensive. A challenge of course, but with these recipes and some simple planning, you can have it all.

Drawing on a variety of cooking styles, especially the ones we know and love best—American, Italian, French, Spanish, Native American—we set out to create low-cost recipes that emphasize plants, healthful oils and sparing use of meat, seafood, salt and sugar. Some are new takes on old favorites. Aiming high for quality and flavor, we cook a dish multiple times to determine the essentials and then distill to its essence. This means fewer ingredients and less time in the kitchen.

You can prepare many of these recipes with pantry basics or easily substitute alternative ingredients. Many are ideal for batch-cooking, can be made in a single pot and freeze well. Even the festive holiday fare and luxurious-tasting treats are simple to prepare and inexpensive.

Two menu plans show you how to turn out several enticing meals based on a single ingredient and how you, too, can cook better and spend less, even with ever-rising food costs. Key recipes provide more tasty ways to enhance kitchen economy. Each ingredient has been priced so you will see the approximate cost per serving and how we can eat for as little as $5 a day per person: spicy lentil soup for about 72¢ a serving, roasted lemon chicken and a side for $1.43, a blackberry-lemon muffin for about 24¢, coconut-chia pudding for 87¢, sweet potato and bean enchiladas for $1.33 a serving. Heartier appetites might count on two or even three servings per person, which still lands in budget-friendly territory.

Consumer reporters, food writers and subscribers to our website have tested our recipes, and when a reporter followed one of our menu plans, cooking on camera every night for a week, he was surprised to have money left over. Even we were surprised by that! On Boston Public Television, the host expressed doubt that our dishes would excite his palate but grabbed a spoon, as our interview ended, and finished off the rum-chocolate dessert we had brought for him to taste.

You'll find affordable splurges like that rum-chocolate ricotta here, along with an authentic, Italian pasta dish you can make in a few minutes with just three pantry ingredients; also, warmly spiced chili with subtle hints of cinnamon and chocolate; and an unusual white lasagne in a luscious sauce of three cheeses, appropriate for your nicest occasions. We've discovered that even the glory of Spanish cooking—paella—can be made inexpensively, and it doesn't take all day either.

We started out developing recipes for delicious, inexpensive meals just to share among ourselves—a widely scattered family longing for more connection. Our cooking experience ranges from avid to professional, but everyone was interested in the challenge of eating well for less. Between us, we've cooked in restaurants in the U.S. and France, tested recipes for well known chefs including Julia Child and written about food and culture. Friends and their families got interested, so we created a website, The Five Dollar Foodie, to exchange ideas and techniques. Now, in response to many requests for a book, we have gathered together over 50 of our best recipes and some exciting new discoveries.

We share, too, what we learned while developing and researching recipes, their origins and nutrition: why one of the oldest health foods on the planet is still one of the best; organic versus conventional ingredients—the clean fifteen and the dirty dozen; when to shop at farmers' markets for bargains; an inexpensive spice to replace saffron that gives genuine flavor to paella; a practical, delightful Native American cooking technique; how to preserve leftover cheese; preparing quick, homemade chicken broth and storing it safely; flavor profiles and flavor affinities; and easy secrets of professional cooks to enhance flavor.

The power of good food to create happiness is, well, almost beyond words. Whether you're cooking every day, a day now and then, for one or many, we are happy to share with you how we learned to cook better, spend less and enjoy more.

A NOTE ON COSTS, INGREDIENTS AND COOKING TIMES

Food costs are based on standard consumer indices and our own personal test shopping at a range of grocery stores, small and large, in varied locales. For detailed costs, down to a teaspoon of olive oil, see thefivedollarfoodie.com. Optional ingredients are not included in pricing. Serving sizes are based on average standards: 2 ounces of pasta, a slice of quiche, an 8-ounce cup of soup or stew, for example.

We cook with a combination of organic and conventional ingredients, relying on the best available information and cost. See the Shopping Tips for more about this. Keep an eye, too, on what is in season, plentiful and grown locally. When organic carrots or apples are half the price of conventional ones—buy them! If your market offers pasta for 99¢ a pound, stock up.

Ingredients: vegetables are assumed to be medium-size unless specified. Carrots, onions and garlic are assumed to be peeled. Spices are ground and herbs are dried, except where noted. Quantities for canned foods, which tend to vary, are rounded: if a packaged coconut milk or can of beans is a few ounces more or less than what a recipe calls for, this won't affect the result in stews, salads, soups and most other dishes. For pastry and cakes though, all ingredients are precisely specified because even a small difference in quantity can be significant.

Preparation and cooking times will vary with kitchen equipment and individual cooks. Our estimates are based on how long it took us and the wonderful testers and website subscribers, who won't let us get away with anything. To all of you, thank you!

WHO WE ARE

The family of five that is the $5 Foodie team want it all—inexpensive food that is healthy, tasty, and leaves a low environmental footprint. The $5 Foodie website and cookbook are the result of their labor of love.

Over five years, Lucy Holland, Carol and Hugo Rizzoli, and Ethan and Amanda Eron shared tips, recipes and meal plans based on a variety of cuisines—American, Native American, Spanish, French and Italian—with the added challenge of cooking for under $5 a day! At first, "it seemed almost impossible," says Carol Rizzoli, "but with time it got easier as we got better at it."

"As a mom of two young children," says Lucy Holland, "I'm interested in cutting not just costs but time when it comes to cooking." As a result the recipes cooked up by the $5 Foodie are not only inexpensive, healthy and tasty, they are also easy to make, quick to cook, and the ingredients can easily be found at a variety of locales.

So who are the people behind the $5 Foodie?

LUCY HOLLAND is the project's co-director, and takes care of developing, testing and photographing the recipes. Her love of cooking developed when she was an art student in Italy and she fell in love with local dishes and the concepts of creating sauces from tomatoes in season and repurposing stale bread into a soup or croutons. When she is not in the kitchen, Lucy teaches art history. She is the author of two books on art for families.

CAROL RIZZOLI enjoys developing, testing and editing recipes for the $5 Foodie. Her memoir with recipes, *The House at Royal Oak*, was honored by the New York Times as one of the best travel books of the year. She is also the creator of *The Artist's Table*, in collaboration with Julia Child and other master chefs. Carol's reviews, essays and profiles have appeared in the Washington Post, Reader's Digest, Smithsonian Magazine, and Victoria, among many other publications. She has given cooking demonstrations and lectures on food and culture.

ETHAN ERON is, along with his sister Lucy, the co-director of the $5 Foodie. Ethan built the website with its community-sharing features and cost-calculator. Ethan is particularly proud of the latter, which, he says, "ensures that our prices remain up-to-date and allows us to search for new ways to save everyone money and continue dining like foodies." He always liked cooking at home and at a trattoria as a student. Currently, when he is not contributing recipes to the project, he works on his software business and surfs in Ocean Beach, California. In 2018, he took himself to France for training at the Cordon Bleu.

AMANDA ERON is a citizen of the world, which has greatly influenced her cooking style. She was smitten with the flavors of Latin America and the Mediterranean when living in Costa Rica, France and Spain. But, she says, "eating out quickly got too expensive for a yoga teacher," so she started recreating the recipes she loved with inexpensive, local ingredients, making them gluten- and dairy-free. She also worked as a sous-chef at a Parisian bistro, tested recipes for two cookbooks, and assisted in giving an artful cooking class at the San Diego Museum of Art.

HUGO RIZZOLI takes his love of cooking from his Italian family background, elucidating recipes passed down from his aunt and grandmother. After training at l'Academie de Cuisine, Hugo ran Seasons, his catering business, and for ten years he and his wife, Carol, owned and cooked for their bed and breakfast on the Chesapeake Bay. Now he keeps a close eye on cooking technique and flavor profiles for the $5 Foodie team. Hugo prides himself on creating recipes "that honor long-held cultural traditions, respect the earth and are healthful as well as affordable." He and Carol live on Cape Cod where Hugo works as an artist.

1 MENUS + SHOPPING TIPS

Planning several meals around a single ingredient is key to eating well on a budget—as is how you shop. This short list of menu-planning ideas and shopping strategies will guide you to creating your own successful, incredibly economical menus and delicious meals.

Two menu plans, each with four very tasty dinners and optional breakfast and lunch suggestions, come in at about $5 a day per person. The goal of menu planning is to make efficient use of your ingredients and to shop accordingly— keys to saving money. Some ingredients appear multiple times in the recipes, and we also suggest substitutions to help your ingredients go further.

The first menu plan is vegetarian, with beans, lentils and sweet potatoes used in a variety of enticing ways. The second menu plan centers around roasting a chicken (Day 1), from which you can turn out three excellent and varied meals for two or more people. You can skip the breakfast and lunch suggestions for a grab-and-go meal, like we often do, or mix and match as you like.

Not planning to cook every day? Many foods can be frozen for later use: from cheese, bacon, tortillas, corn, bread and milk to cooked chicken, chicken bones for broth and even fresh herbs, wrapped in plastic or wax paper and stored in an airtight container. Herbs, too, are so adaptable that you can usually substitute one for another, depending on what you have at hand.

These menus are intended to provide ideas and, we hope, inspiration for creating plans according to your own preferences and individual nutritional needs. Costs will vary by season, by region and from one store to another.

MENU 1 PLANT-BASED

This plant-rich plan starts with cooking a big pot of beans, which can be used in multiple recipes through the week, and includes two easy lentil dishes—all good-for-you and full of veggies and protein. Plus, your weekly cost comes in well under $5 a day per person thanks to these cost-effective staples. You can easily substitute another type of bean, such as pinto, for the black beans, and red or brown lentils can be interchangeable with cook-time adjustments. Note: buy spinach once, for the orzo, and use it again in the fried rice or serve with the sweet potato chili. Zucchini also makes more than one appearance.

DAY 1   Latin-Style Beans and Rice (37¢)

BREAKFAST AND LUNCH IDEAS:
Coconut Chia Pudding (87¢) with 2 eggs (add 50¢)
Lemon-Spinach Orzo* ($1.00)

DAY 2   Ginger Curried Lentils (71¢)

BREAKFAST AND LUNCH IDEAS:
Almond-Vanilla Granola (83¢) with yogurt (add 99¢)
Veggie Fried Rice (71¢)

DAY 3   Easy Black Bean Posole (83¢)

BREAKFAST AND LUNCH IDEAS:
Zucchini and Cheese Omelet ($1.90)
Quinoa and Lentil Salad ($1.53)

DAY 4   Sweet Potato Chili (90¢)

BREAKFAST AND LUNCH IDEAS:
Oatmeal with Apple and Apricots (76¢)
Zucchini, Corn and Black Bean Fritters ($1.21)

MENU 2 with Roasted Chicken

This meal plan centers around roasting a chicken, from which you can make 3 good meals for 2 or more people, including Brunswick Stew and Quick Chicken Broth for Greens and Rice Soup. In this plan, ingredients such as potatoes, lettuce, eggs and cheese, in addition to the chicken, come into play more than once.

DAY 1

Lemon and Garlic Roasted Chicken with Sweet Potatoes ($1.43)

Breakfast and lunch ideas:
Blackberry-Lemon Muffin (27¢) with fresh fruit (add 79¢)
Brie Panini with Fresh Pear and Red Fruit Jam ($1.36)

DAY 2

Potatoes Gratin with Glazed Carrots ($1.92)

Breakfast and lunch ideas:
Almond-Vanilla Granola (83¢) with yogurt (add 99¢)
Olive and Herb Tuna Wrap ($1.27)

DAY 3

Brunswick Stew (95¢)

Breakfast and lunch ideas:
Zucchini and Cheese Omelet ($1.90)
Chickpea-Mint Salad ($1.95)

DAY 4

Greens and Rice Soup ($1.66)

Breakfast and lunch ideas:
Quesadillas with Bacon and Scallion (92¢)
Asparagus and Eggs with Creamy Lemon Sauce* ($1.16)

*See **thefivedollarfoodie.com** for these recipes and many more choices to make your budget work.

HOW TO SHOP

Food shopping is not only easier with a plan in mind but more economical, too, and shopping when you are not hungry lets you make better choices! More hints for getting the most out of your food budget:

1. **Find discount grocery stores** in your area. Not all stores price identical products the same.

2. **If an item is on sale, buy larger quantities** and store or freeze extras.

3. **Know how to substitute one ingredient for another.** If a green or herb you think you need is pricey that day, go with one that is less expensive. Replace escarole with spinach, chard or kale. Replace a $4 herb with one that is 69¢ and will give just as much flavor to your recipe. Dill, chive, mint from the backyard and many other possibilities will be delish in salads and wraps.

4. **Shop late in the day at the local farm market**, when bargains can be found as dealers want to unload produce that may not be in peak condition by the next day, or they just have too much of it.

5. **Ask at the farm market for "seconds" on produce** like apples and tomatoes. They're usually kept out of sight, but if you say you want to make a pie or tomato sauce, the vendor is likely to come up with a basketful at a fraction of the price of the best produce, and be happy to sell it to you.

6. **Buying in bulk from the bins** that some stores have can save a lot of money. Making your own granola, according to our recipe, can save you a bundle over buying the premade product—and it tastes better of course.

7. **Know when not to shop!** This is when you have leftover food at home that can probably be turned into an excellent meal. See the recipe for Farmhouse Sausage and Vegetable Soup as an example.

WHEN TO BUY ORGANIC?

We can sometimes find organic ingredients for the same price or less than their conventional counterparts. If you plan to use organic ingredients exclusively, count on adding 20% or more to our estimated costs. These guidelines* show when it is wise to purchase organic produce. Often, we weigh the cost of the item and its "clean factor" when deciding whether to make a purchase. Another option is frozen organic produce, which can be less expensive than fresh because it is less perishable.

THE CLEAN FIFTEEN Avocado, corn, pineapple, onion, papaya, sweet peas (frozen), eggplant, asparagus, cauliflower, cantaloupe, broccoli, mushrooms, cabbage, honeydew melon, kiwi

THE DIRTY DOZEN Strawberries, spinach, kale, nectarines, apples, grapes, peaches, cherries, pears, tomatoes, celery, bell and hot peppers

*Source: © Environmental Working Group at ewg.org. Reproduced with permission.

2 KEYS TO FLAVOR

Seemingly small touches can make a big difference in the flavor of whatever you are cooking. Creating fantastic flavor with little effort or cost: it's all part of cooking better, spending less and— most of all—enjoying more. Here are our top five:

1. **A chef's best friend is. . . salt.** But you don't need a lot of it to add sparkle to your cooking. Make it a habit to taste your soup, sauce, stew and other savory dishes, season with salt and pepper if needed—then taste again.

2. **Lemon** A few drops of lemon juice bring zest to a dish that may taste good but just needs a little something more. We learned this trick from Julia Child, who often added lemon juice even to her most elaborate sauces.

3. **Nutmeg and allspice** are wonderful enhancers of flavor, by the pinch or in generous quantity, depending on what you are cooking or baking. Nutmeg, for example, flavors our vegetarian Bolognese sauce and allspice adds a subtle note to our chocolate-orange banana bread.

4. **Contrasts of color and texture** also contribute to taste and flavor. With a pale-hued pasta or potato dish, consider adding a bright green salad or go for a knockout side of purple cabbage with orange carrots. Add crunch and nutrition to grain dishes, as we do with seeds or nuts.

5. **Sweet, sour, bitter and salty** are the four basic tastes we perceive, and a dish that balances these will be very delicious. A seemingly simple stew, our Cuban Picadillo includes a balance of raisins (sweet), vinegar and tomatoes (sour) and olives (salty). Our Vietnamese Sweet-Sour-Salty Noodle Salad includes fish sauce which gives it umami, sometimes considered a fifth taste.

3 PANTRY

With pantry basics you can easily turn out delectable, inexpensive dishes like flavorful White Bean Soup, Ginger Curried Lentils, Potatoes Gratin, an easy Black Bean Posole with authentic Mexican flavor and more. Some of the recipes are based entirely on canned, jarred or dried staples, and many adapt well to alternative ingredients. The very simplest, Spaghetti Aglio e Olio—a staple in Italian home kitchens—requires just 3 basic ingredients and 12 minutes to cook.

Potatoes Gratin with Glazed Carrots, page 24

WHITE BEAN SOUP

So tasty and nutritious! White cannellini beans simmered with garlic, a splash of olive oil and a hint of rosemary are a Tuscan favorite. With whatever white beans and herbs you have, the soup will be wonderful. Full of healthful fiber, protein and potassium in addition to iron and calcium, beans make an easy one-pot meal, all for about 55¢ a serving. Optional kale can be tossed in for the last few minutes of cooking for extra nutrients. Along with crusty bread and a wedge of cheese, call it supper.

MAKES 7 SERVINGS | PREP TIME: 15 MINUTES | COOK TIME: 20 MINUTES | 55¢ / SERVING

3 tablespoons olive oil
1 onion, chopped (about ¾ cup)
1 carrot, chopped
2 garlic cloves, chopped
1 tablespoon tomato paste (or ketchup)
salt and pepper
4 cups water
3 15-ounce cans cannellini beans, drained (or equivalent quantity of dried beans, cooked according to package instructions)
1 bay leaf
1 teaspoon thyme
½ teaspoon rosemary (or 1 teaspoon oregano or basil)
* optional: 2 cups chopped fresh kale; ½ lemon; extra olive oil and fresh rosemary for garnish

1. In a large soup pot, heat the olive oil over medium-low heat, adding the onion, carrot, garlic and tomato paste (or ketchup), along with a pinch of salt and several of black pepper. Stir, cover and cook for about 2 minutes.

2. Raise the heat to medium high and add the water, beans, bay leaf, thyme and rosemary (basil or oregano). Cover and maintain an easy simmer for about 12-15 minutes.

3. Remove pot from the heat and mash some of the beans—the bottom of a wine bottle does the job—or place about ⅓ of the soup in a blender or food processor and carefully puree until it's silky. To prevent splashing of the hot liquid, hold a dish towel tightly over the blender or processor lid, or allow the soup to cool first. The mashing gives a more rustic effect; the blender, a creamier result.

4. Return soup to the pot and stir. Taste for seasoning and add more salt and pepper as needed. If you are including kale, add it now and cook a few minutes until it has softened. A squeeze of fresh lemon at the end of the cooking adds a bright note.

5. To serve, ladle the soup into bowls and decorate with an optional herb sprig and a small swirl of olive oil.

NOTES:
☐ Replace cannellini beans with great northern or navy beans, even chickpeas, depending what you have.
☐ For another rich layer of flavor, add ⅓ cup diced ham to the pot to simmer along with the beans.

OLIVE AND HERB TUNA WRAP

Incredibly easy, these zesty wraps are ready in less than ten minutes. Flecks of olive and herb balance the flavors, along with a grating of fresh onion and a dash of honey. Tuna is an excellent source of protein— here 15 grams per serving— as well as B vitamins and omega-3 fatty acids. Plus it's so inexpensive when you shop carefully. "Light" tuna, which is more healthful than "white" tuna, also costs less.

MAKES 2 SERVINGS | PREP TIME: 7 MINUTES | $1.27 / SERVING

1 5-ounce can tuna
4 tablespoons mayonnaise
2 tablespoons relish
1 tablespoon onion, grated
1 teaspoon vinegar
1 teaspoon honey
6 olives, chopped
1 tablespoon fresh dill or mint, finely chopped
2 tortillas (use corn or spelt tortillas for a gluten-free version)
4 lettuce leaves

1. Drain tuna and place in a small mixing bowl. Add the mayonnaise, relish, grated onion, vinegar, honey, olives and fresh herb. Stir with a fork until well combined.

2. Place each tortilla on a plate. Layer two lettuce leaves on each tortilla, then top with tuna salad. Firmly roll up each tortilla. Alternately, the tuna salad can be refrigerated and the wraps assembled later.

NOTES:
☐ If using corn tortillas, heat them for a minute in a hot skillet or for 20 seconds in the microwave to prevent breaking.

☐ Dried herbs can be substituted for fresh ones; just use less: here, a teaspoon of dried dill or mint.

GINGER CURRIED LENTILS

Red lentils turn saffron-hued in their brief cooking time, blending with a delicate balance of ginger, onion, garlic, curry and—surprise—fresh lemon slices. But any lentils you have will do. Fragrant basmati rice complements the Indian flavor profile, though standard white or brown rice can be used. Lentils, an ancient source of healthful nutrition dating back thousands of years, are still one of the best. Rich in iron and other nutrients, lentils provide 12 grams of protein in each serving. Enjoy them with mint yogurt, crispy onions, fresh chutney—or all three.

Makes 4 servings | Prep time: 15 minutes | Cook time: 25 minutes | 71 ¢ / serving

1 small onion, diced
3 garlic cloves
½ teaspoon ginger (or ½ inch fresh ginger, peeled and minced)
3 tablespoons oil (or half oil, half butter)
2 teaspoons curry powder
1 cup red lentils (dried)
2 ¼ cups water
salt and pepper
½ lemon, thinly sliced in rounds, then halved
1 cup rice (white or brown)

> 6 ounces plain yogurt
> 1 sprig fresh mint, finely chopped (or ½ teaspoon dried mint)
> salt

FOR THE CRISPY ONIONS:
> 1 large onion, thinly sliced
> 1 tablespoon oil

OPTIONAL FRESH FRUIT CHUTNEY:
> ½ mango, peeled and cut into bite-size pieces (or ½ cup of other fresh fruit like apple, banana or pineapple)
> ½ jalapeño pepper, seeds removed and finely diced, or ⅛ teaspoon cayenne pepper
> 1 teaspoon vinegar (preferably rice wine vinegar)
> 2 teaspoons onion, minced
> salt
> ⅛ red bell pepper, minced

1. Place the onion, garlic, ginger, oil (plus butter, if using) and curry powder in a large saucepan over medium heat and stir until the onion begins to soften, about 1 minute. Add the lentils, 2 ¼ cups water, ¾ teaspoon salt and pepper to taste along with the lemon slices. Bring to a boil, then lower heat. Cover the pot and simmer for about 15 minutes, until the lentils are tender. If they look dry, add a bit more water as they finish cooking.

2. Meanwhile set the rice to cook in another saucepan, following package instructions.

3. While the lentils and rice cook, prepare the yogurt sauce: place yogurt in a serving dish and stir with a fork to smooth it, adding a little water as needed. Stir in the mint and ¼ teaspoon salt.

4. For the crispy onions: in a medium-size frying pan, place the thinly-sliced large onion and 1 tablespoon oil and cook over medium-high heat until onion slices are crisp and browned, about 5 minutes. If the oil starts to smoke, remove pan from the burner and lower heat before you resume frying. With a slotted spoon, remove onions to a paper towel to absorb excess oil before placing them in a serving dish.

5. Optional fresh fruit chutney: Stir together all ingredients in a serving dish.

6. To serve, spoon the rice onto a plate and surround with the lentils. Top with the mint yogurt, crispy onions and optional chutney, or place each accompaniment in a serving dish to pass around the table.

NOTES:

☐ Lentils range in color from red, green, orange and yellow, to brown and black. You can use any type in this dish, but note that cooking times will vary. Red lentils are mild and sweet in flavor, while some brown varieties are nuttier. Others, like French green lentils, hold their shape well when cooked and are a good choice for salads.

☐ A relish or chutney is traditional at Indian meals, and not all are laboriously cooked for hours. This quickly made and lively accompaniment adds little (about 13¢) to the cost per serving.

☐ When preparing a jalapeño for chutney, be sure to remove the seeds before mincing the pepper as the seeds can be fiery.

Potatoes Gratin with Glazed Carrots

The potato is a great staple. For centuries it's been known that potatoes contain most of the vitamins and minerals (vitamin C, B6, potassium, magnesium and iron, to name a few) needed for sustenance, while being extremely affordable. Here potatoes are dressed up in a classic gratin with onion and cheese. Round out dinner with glazed carrots, below, or a simple green salad.

Makes 2 servings | Prep time: 20 minutes | Cook time: 45 minutes (total active time: 25 minutes) | $1.92 / serving

1 tablespoon oil (or butter)
2 large potatoes, sliced thinly (about ⅛-inch thick)
¾ onion, chopped into small pieces
salt and pepper
nutmeg
1 cup swiss cheese (or cheddar), grated
1 cup milk

FOR THE GLAZED CARROTS:

> 4 carrots
> 2 tablespoons honey (or sugar)
> *optional: 1 tablespoon frozen orange juice concentrate (or juice of half an orange and its zest)

1. Preheat the oven to 400 degrees. Lightly coat a small pie pan or baking dish with a film of butter or oil (a smaller pan will make a thicker gratin). Place a layer of potatoes in the pan, sprinkle with onion, salt and pepper to taste, a pinch or two of nutmeg and a layer of cheese. Repeat the layering until all ingredients are used, finishing with cheese on top.

2. Pour milk over the potatoes and bake for about 45 minutes. The gratin is done when it bubbles, the top layer of cheese turns light brown and the potatoes are soft when tested with a fork.

3. While the gratin bakes, place the carrots in a pan with enough water to cover them. Bring to a boil, cover the pan and cook for about 5 minutes or until the carrots are almost tender. Drain off the water and add, to taste: 2 tablespoons honey (or sugar), salt and pepper. If you have frozen orange juice concentrate, toss a tablespoon into the pan for extra flavor; or try squeezes of fresh orange and zest. Cook the carrots over low heat for about 5 more minutes until they are glazed and can be cut with a fork.

4. To serve, cut sections of the gratin and place on a plate along with the vegetable.

EASY BLACK BEAN POSOLE

Too good to be true? Only until you try this rustic, healthful vegetarian stew, or posole, with authentic Mexican flavor. Start to finish, cooking takes half an hour, and you can make it all in one pot. Chewy, fiber-rich hominy (corn) and black beans play off the tangy salsa, green chiles and lime to create a warm flavor blend and varied textures. Hominy, by the way, is simply kernels of corn that have been soaked in limewater and hulled. Most of the ingredients are pantry staples, dried, jarred or canned. Substitutions are easy: use water in place of vegetable broth; omit the hominy or green chilies; swap another vegetable like zucchini, carrot, squash or spinach for the bell pepper. Topped with optional cheese, avocado and/ or tortilla chips, this is a true crowd-pleaser.

1 onion, chopped
1 red bell pepper, chopped
*½ cup mushrooms, chopped (optional)
1 tablespoon oil
3 garlic cloves, minced
2 cups vegetable broth (or water)
1 15-ounce can black beans, drained
1 15-ounce can hominy (or corn)
1 cup green salsa, mild or hot
1 4-ounce can diced green chiles
2 tablespoons lime juice
1 tablespoon flour (or 1 teaspoon cornstarch dissolved in water for gluten-free version)
salt and pepper
* optional garnishes: 2 tablespoons heavy cream, 1 diced avocado, ½ cup shredded cheddar or jack cheese, 6 ounces tortilla chips

1. In a good-sized soup pot, sauté the onion, bell pepper, and optional mushrooms in oil over medium heat for 2 minutes or until just softened. Add the garlic and sauté another minute.

2. Add the vegetable broth (or water), black beans, hominy, salsa, green chiles and lime juice, and stir. Reduce heat to medium-low and stir in the flour to thicken the broth. Simmer for about 15 minutes until the flavors meld and the stew is heated through. Season with salt and pepper to taste. You can leave it on the stove on lowest heat for over an hour and it only gets better.

3. Stir in the heavy cream if using just before serving. Ladle the posole into bowls and top with optional avocado, shredded cheese or tortilla chips.

NOTES:
☐ Subtitute red salsa for the green if you want to try a different version of this dish.
☐ You can use dried beans and dried hominy, if you prefer, soaked and cooked according to package directions.
☐ For a vegan version, omit the cream or add coconut milk instead; for a gluten-free version omit the flour or use one teaspoon of cornstarch dissolved in a few tablespoons of water.
☐ For the red bell pepper, you can substitute green, yellow or orange peppers, carrot, or zucchini.
☐ Store any leftovers in an airtight container in the refrigerator, or freeze.

Spaghetti Aglio e Olio

A little garlic, oil, pasta—and you're all set. Subtly delicious, this simple dish captures the essence of Italian home cooking. Both beginning cooks and the experienced will enjoy turning out spaghetti tossed with garlic oil. Our own pantry is never without these three basic ingredients. Tradition calls for spaghetti, but linguine or other long, narrow pasta will be just fine. Salad makes a nice accompaniment.

Makes 4 servings | Prep time: 5 minutes | Cook time: 12 minutes | 26 ¢ / serving

    3 garlic cloves
    ¼ cup olive oil, plus extra to taste
    salt and pepper
    pinch of red pepper flakes
    ½ pound spaghetti

1. Bring a pot of salted water to a boil over high heat.

2. Meanwhile prepare the garlic oil by crushing the peeled garlic cloves (a knife handle can be used for this). Place them in a small pan with ¼ cup olive oil and slowly cook over low heat for about 3-5 minutes, until the garlic is softened and lightly colored. Remove the garlic pieces from the oil or leave them in. Add salt and pepper to taste along with a good pinch of red pepper flakes.

3. Boil the spaghetti until it is tender but al dente. Drain the pasta and return it to the pot. Toss it well with the garlic oil, adding a little extra oil if desired, and serve.

NOTES:

☐ You can drain the pasta water into the serving dishes to warm them, then tip the water out before serving the spaghetti.

☐ Delightful add-ons to the oil and garlic include lemon zest, fennel seed, minced fresh herbs or whatever else appeals.

☐ The flavor hound who tested this family favorite prefers roasting 8 whole garlic cloves in the oil, at 350 degrees, for about 5-8 minutes and garnishing the pasta with the roasted garlic along with some parsley and parmesan. *Va bene*!

4 ONE POT

. . . or pan does it all. Every culture values one-pot cooking as these satisfying favorites from American, Mexican, Asian, Italian and French traditions show— from Classic Onion Soup to a luscious Lime-Coconut Curry with Chicken and Brunswick Stew, an American classic that dates to colonial times and earlier. We've served it up almost forever on plain and fancy occasions—and you probably will, too. These good-for-you stews and soups hold well and even improve by the next day, if there's any left.

Classic Onion Soup, page 40

BRUNSWICK STEW

Corn, tomatoes and lima beans simmered together with chicken and potatoes make a hearty dinner, with short prep and cooking times. Brunswick Stew invites gathering around to serve yourself from the pot, and colorful vegetables, fresh or frozen, shine here with light seasoning, the tang of Worcestershire sauce and lemon. This stew satisfies good appetites, too. Fine just off the fire—or the next day—it dates to colonial times and before. Native Americans stewed corn and beans together with wild game, and in various forms it's been enjoyed ever since.

2 chicken breast halves, bone in (about 1 ¼ pounds) or 4 chicken thighs
1 ¼ cups water
1 bay leaf
salt and pepper
8 ounces lima beans (fresh, frozen or cooked dried limas)
8 ounces corn kernels
1 15-ounce can diced tomatoes with juice
1 onion, chopped
2 potatoes (about ½ pound), peeled or not and cut into bite-size pieces
1 teaspoon thyme
1 tablespoon Worcestershire sauce
2 tablespoons flour
*optional: substitute leftover cooked chicken plus 1 cup chicken broth for uncooked chicken; for the sauce, juice of ½ lemon and 2 tablespoons butter

1. In a medium-size soup pot, place the chicken, 1 cup of water, bay leaf, ¼ teaspoon salt and black pepper to taste. Bring to a simmer, cover and cook about 20 minutes, until the chicken is done (opaque and no longer pink when you cut into the thickest part). While the chicken simmers, prepare the vegetables and assemble the remaining ingredients.

2. Remove chicken from the pot, placing it on a plate to cool. Add the lima beans, corn, tomatoes with juice, onion, potatoes, thyme and Worcestershire sauce to the pot and simmer, covered. As the vegetables cook, shred chicken into bite-size pieces (discard skin and bones) and return it to the pot.

3. Continue simmering the stew, covered, until the vegetables are nicely tender, about 20 minutes more.

4. To thicken the sauce, use a fork to stir flour into ¼ cup of water and blend the mixture until it's smooth. Then stir blended flour into the stew and simmer for a couple of minutes. The sauce should be thick enough to lightly coat a spoon. Optional: squeeze lemon juice into the stew and stir in butter. Taste and season with more salt, pepper and Worcestershire if you like.

NOTES:

☐ You can prepare this recipe with previously cooked chicken and chicken broth. Place the broth in a pot and proceed with adding vegetables in step 2.

☐ Bone-in chicken produces a rich-tasting broth. But you can use boneless, skinless chicken if you prefer, or a combination of white and dark meat including drumsticks.

☐ The butter gives added richness—"mouth-feel"—to the stew. As professional chefs know, fat is a great carrier of flavor. A second pro tip for sparking flavor is lemon juice. And third, tasting is essential to cooking with flavor. Taste along the way, once or more, for salt and pepper.

CHILI WITH CINNAMON AND CACAO

The classic Mexican pairing of chile pepper, tomato and unsweetened chocolate gives warm flavor you have to taste to understand. Cook and feast in an hour or keep the chili over a night or two and the flavor only gets better. It's mild enough for gringo-mouths, but if you like more fire, splash it with green and red pepper sauces. Along with optional scallion, sour cream and avocado, smoky, chipotle hot sauce is especially good. You can also make a vegan version of this chili by substituting sweet potato for the beef, which also cuts the cost in half.

MAKES 5 SERVINGS | PREP TIME: 5 MINUTES | COOK TIME: 25 MINUTES | $1.85 / SERVING

1 onion, chopped
1 tablespoon oil (mildly flavored, like canola or safflower)
½ pound ground beef
1 ½ teaspoons cumin
½ teaspoon cinnamon
salt and pepper
1 28-ounce can crushed tomatoes
⅔ cup water
4 ounces canned green chiles, diced
2 tablespoons cocoa powder (unsweetened) or cacao powder
1 15-ounce can black beans
1 15-ounce can kidney beans
5 tortillas
*optional garnishes: 5 ounces sour cream, 2 scallions, 1 diced avocado, green and red pepper sauces

1. In a medium-size stew pot, place the onion and oil and sauté 4-5 minutes or until the onion starts to brown slightly. Add the beef, cumin, cinnamon, ½ teaspoon salt and pepper to taste. Turn up the heat and use a fork to break the meat apart as it lightly browns. This should take 5 minutes or less.

2. Add tomatoes, ⅔ cup water, green chiles and cocoa powder to the meat and onion mixture. Stir, cover and simmer 5 minutes.

3. Drain the beans of their liquid and add them to the pot. Simmer 10 minutes or longer. Taste and adjust seasonings.

4. To serve, tuck a folded tortilla into each bowl, ladle on the chili and garnish with an optional spoonful of sour cream on top of each serving, then the scallion and avocado. Pass around the hot sauces!

NOTES:

☐ Cocoa and cacao powder are both derived from the bean of the plant Theobroma cacao. Cacao powder is raw; more readily available and less expensive, cocoa powder is roasted.

☐ You can use half a fresh jalapeño pepper in place of the canned green chiles if you prefer. Just take care to remove the seeds before mincing it and do taste for heat, using more or less accordingly. Chile peppers are unpredictable!

☐ This recipe is also delicious without meat. Substitue a cubed sweet potato for the beef and add 20-30 minutes to the cook time in step 2. You may also add a tablespoon of chili powder to give rich flavor to the vegetarian version. For a vegan version, omit the sour cream.

FARMHOUSE SAUSAGE AND VEGETABLE SOUP

Everyone is hungry and the fridge is almost empty. This awesome accidental soup—it's thick, more like stew, and full-flavored—surprised even the cook when it was ready. From the fridge came: 4 carrots, 3 sausages, 2 potatoes, 1 carton of chicken broth, some leftover marinara sauce and a takeout box of rice. With a little oil, garlic and dried herbs, we were enjoying a fantastic supper 30 minutes later. Best about this approach: the soup can be made with pretty much any veggies and protein you have around. Our ingredients suggested Provence, so we chose oregano, basil, thyme, garlic and fennel for a pleasing, consistent flavor profile.

3 precooked sausages (chicken and apple, spicy Italian or pork)
2 tablespoons olive oil
6 garlic cloves, minced
4 cups chicken broth (or a combination of broth and water)
⅔ cup water
4 carrots, sliced lengthwise, then halved
1 cup tomato sauce
2 potatoes (white or sweet), cut in small cubes
⅓ cup white rice (uncooked)
1 teaspoon oregano
1 teaspoon basil
1 teaspoon thyme
salt and pepper
*optional: 1 teaspoon fennel seed

1. Slice the sausages into ¼-inch rounds. Heat the oil in a medium-size pot until it shimmers and add the sausages. Sauté them until lightly browned, about 3 minutes.

2. Add all the other ingredients to the pot along with salt and pepper to taste. Bring the soup to a simmer. Cover the pot and simmer over low heat until the vegetables are tender and the soup is nicely thickened, about 20 minutes. If too thick, add a little extra water. The soup also benefits from "resting"—sitting off the heat for 5-10 minutes before serving, but this isn't necessary.

3. Taste and adjust the seasonings. Soup's on!

NOTE:
☐ If you have leftover cooked rice on hand, you can substitute one cup of cooked rice for ⅓ cup uncooked rice and omit the extra ⅔ cup of water.

LIME-COCONUT CURRY WITH CHICKEN

Green curry with lime is one of those dishes—when made this way—that leaves guests swooning and demanding the recipe. It takes a little longer and has a few more ingredients than many of our recipes, but is so worth it. Tender, bright green vegetables and the fragrance of fresh cilantro enhance gentle zings of spice and pepper, coconut milk and a richly flavored chicken broth in this curried soup. Yes, a key to truly memorable green curry is making the broth from scratch, which provides the deep flavor. But before you give up in despair and order a pizza, hear us out on the chicken broth! It can be made with leftover chicken bones and vegetables, so it is a great use of staples that would otherwise perish from neglect in the back of the fridge (see Quick Chicken Broth in the Key Recipes). Of course you can always use packaged broth enhanced with chicken bouillon (or chicken base), but if you give homemade a try, you won't regret it. For hearty appetites, serve the curry with jasmine rice.

Makes 6 servings | Prep time: 10 minutes | Cook time: 35 minutes (add 30 min for homemade broth) | $1.76 / serving

1 potato, diced
½ onion, diced
2 tablespoons oil (canola or other mildly flavored oil)
½ pound chicken breasts or thighs, boneless and skinless
4 cups chicken broth
1 tablespoon green curry paste (or more, to taste)
1 large green chile pepper (a mild variety, like poblano or anaheim), minced
1 13-ounce can coconut milk
2 limes, juiced
salt
4 cups broccoli, snow peas, green beans or other green vegetables
1 cup fresh cilantro, chopped
1 cup green onion, chopped
*optional: 1 chicken bouillon cube or chicken base (if not using homemade chicken broth); 1 ½ cups jasmine rice, cooked according to package instructions; 1 lime, cut in wedges to garnish

1. In a medium-size frying pan, sauté the diced potato and onion in 1 tablespoon oil over medium-high heat, stirring occasionally. Cook until lightly browned and tender, about 6 minutes, and set them aside.

2. Add another tablespoon of oil to the pan and sear the chicken until light brown on one side, about 4 minutes. Turn the chicken, lower heat, cover the pan and cook about 7 minutes more, until the chicken is cooked through. Remove to a plate, and with two forks pull meat apart to shred it into bite-size pieces. The chicken should still be tender and moist on the inside—you will cook it further in step 4, so don't worry if it seems slightly underdone now (it's done when no pink color remains at the center).

3. In a medium-size soup pot, place the chicken broth, curry paste and green chile and turn heat to medium-high. Also add the (optional) bouillon cube (or equivalent roasted chicken base, usually 1 teaspoon) to enhance flavor of packaged broth, stirring until it dissolves.

4. Next, add to the pot the coconut milk, lime juice, cooked potato and onion, 1 teaspoon salt and the cooked, shredded chicken. Bring to a low simmer and cook for about 2 minutes. Remove stem ends from snow peas or beans; cut broccoli into bite-size florets. At the last minute before serving, add the vegetables to the pot. The curry is ready when the vegetables are just tender but still bright green. (Covering the pot or overcooking will cause them to discolor.)

5. Serve the curry hot and garnish each bowl with fresh cilantro, green onion and optional lime wedge. If serving with rice, mound half a cup in the center of the soup bowl and spoon the curry around it, then garnish.

NOTES:

☐ If a milder curry is desired, discard the seeds and white interior membrane of the green chile pepper.

☐ This is a light curry that is broth-based. If you prefer a richer, thicker curry, more of a stew, and are in the mood to splurge, you can reduce the chicken broth to 4 ounces (or omit it entirely), increase the quantity of chicken to ¾ pound, add extra green curry paste and use 2 cans of regular, full-fat coconut milk.

CLASSIC ONION SOUP

We love this French classic anytime but especially on cold winter nights. The aroma of beef broth complements caramelized onions and melted gruyere (if you can't find an inexpensive one, you can use swiss cheese instead). Onions are so flavorful and good for you—they are loaded with vitamin C, flavonoids and healthful phytochemicals. Julia Child inspired our recipe, and we don't think she would mind a few cost- and time-saving shortcuts, like adding water to the beef stock, cutting down the simmer time and repurposing our stale French bread here. This soup is also excellent to freeze (before garnishing with the toasted bread) for another day—or night. Onion soup, after all, became legendary in Paris for late evenings out on the town.

SERVING MAKES 8 SERVINGS | PREP TIME: 10 MINUTES | COOK TIME: 1 HOUR (TOTAL ACTIVE TIME: 40 MINUTES) | $1.86 / SERVING

6 cups onions, sliced thinly
3 tablespoons oil (or butter)
1 teaspoon sugar
salt and pepper
3 tablespoons flour
½ cup white wine
4 cups beef broth
4 cups water
1 baguette (about 10 ounces), sliced in rounds
8 ounces gruyere cheese (or swiss), grated
*optional: 3 tablespoons brandy

1. In a large covered saucepan, cook the onions in oil (or butter) slowly over low heat until they are softened, about 10 minutes. Uncover, sprinkle in sugar and ¾ teaspoon salt. Cook over medium-high heat until browned, about 20 minutes, stirring every few minutes. The sugar helps caramelize the onions to a rich brown color. Then add the flour and stir for a few more minutes.

2. Remove the pan from heat. Slowly and carefully pour in the wine, beef broth and water. Add salt and pepper to taste. Reduce heat to low and simmer for about 30 minutes. If you're short on time, you can simmer less, or let it simmer longer to develop even more flavors. Add the optional brandy just before serving.

3. Meanwhile preheat the oven to 350 degrees. Lay out the baguette rounds in a single layer on a sheet pan and scatter half the cheese over the rounds. Bake them for about 10-15 minutes, until the cheese is melted and the bread lightly browned.

4. Ladle the soup into bowls, stir in the remaining grated cheese and top with 2-3 bread rounds.

VELVET CORN CHOWDER

So creamy, this chowder is actually good for you. Low in fat, it's made with little salt and no dairy! Thanks to Oprah herself, we've been enjoying it for years. Now it's time to share our vegan take. Go for it when there's fresh corn in the markets, though frozen corn works well, too, and our rendition is lightly scented with one of our favorite spices, nutmeg or allspice, and fresh dill or whatever herb you have. We almost always have mint, which is delightful.

MAKES 4 SERVINGS | PREP TIME: 20 MINUTES | COOK TIME: 30 MINUTES | 48 ¢ / SERVING

3 cups corn kernels (fresh or frozen)
½ medium onion, sliced
1 tablespoon olive oil
2 ¾ cups water
salt and pepper
pinches of red pepper flakes
¼ teaspoon thyme
pinches of nutmeg or allspice
½ green or red bell pepper, minced
*optional garnishes: fresh dill, mint, parsley or other herb

1. If using fresh corn, you'll need about three ears. Husk the corn, remove the silk, and with a sharp knife slice the kernels from the cob into a bowl. Then scrape the cob vertically with the knife to extract the remaining "milky" corn and add it to the bowl.

2. In a medium-size soup pot, sauté the onion in oil for 2-3 minutes, until it softens. Add 2 cups of corn and cook for a minute or more.

3. Next, add the water, ⅛ teaspoon salt and as much black and red pepper as you like (2 or more pinches of red pepper if you want a little heat); also add the thyme and a generous pinch or two of nutmeg or allspice. Stir, cover and simmer for about 20 minutes, or until the corn is quite soft. Using a fork, test it by mashing a few kernels against the side of the pot.

4. Puree the soup in a blender or food processor until it is silky and return it to the pot. Add the last cup of corn, taste the soup for seasoning and add more as you like. If the soup seems too thick, add a little more water.

5. Add the bell pepper now and simmer for a few minutes more until the pepper is softened. Ladle the chowder into bowls and garnish with the optional fresh herb and an extra flourish of nutmeg.

NOTE:
☐ Chowder is so fine on its own, or you can choose to make it a more substantial meal with garlic croutons, crumbled bacon, diced ham, even clams, crab or shrimp—whatever's in season if you catch you own, as we do on Cape Cod.

GREENS AND RICE SOUP

The sum here is much more than the parts: a rosy, aromatic broth with garlic, nutmeg, arborio rice and dark greens. Arborio with escarole is wonderful, but you can use other kinds of rice successfully and a variety of leafy greens. Topped with melting parmesan or romano cheese, it makes a delish supper. This is also a super-economical way to turn out a meal from leftover chicken bones by making your own Quick Chicken Broth (see the Key Recipes), though packaged chicken broth can be used. For a very excellent vegetarian version, spike vegetable broth with a good squeeze of lemon juice.

MAKES 6 SERVINGS | PREP TIME: 10 MINUTES | COOK TIME: 20 MINUTES (ADD 30 MINUTES IF PREPARING HOMEMADE BROTH) | $1.66 / SERVING

3 tablespoons olive oil
6 garlic cloves
2 tablespoons tomato paste (or ketchup)
4 cups packaged chicken broth + 2 ½ cups water (or 6 ½ cups homemade chicken broth)
¾ cup arborio rice (or other rice, white or brown)
12-16 ounces dark, leafy greens (like spinach, escarole, chard or kale), chopped
salt and pepper
¾ cup parmesan, romano or pecorino cheese, grated
*optional: pinches of nutmeg

1. If preparing homemade broth, see our Quick Chicken Broth method. For packaged chicken or vegetable broth, skip to step 2.

2. Add the oil and garlic cloves to a medium-size soup pot. Cook them over low heat until softened, about 2 minutes. Stir in the tomato paste (or substitute ketchup).

3. Add 6 ½ cups of homemade chicken broth (or 4 cups packaged chicken broth + 2 ½ cups of water) and bring to a boil. Place rice and pinches of salt and pepper to taste in the pot, cover and cook over medium-low heat for about 7 minutes (if using brown rice, see note below). You want the rice to be just slightly underdone at this point. Add the greens (except spinach), simmer the soup, covered, for about 5 minutes more, until the greens are tender and the rice has given the soup creaminess. If using spinach, just add it for the last minute.

4. This is a thick soup though if it seems too thick, thin with a little water. Check the seasoning but go easy on salt, because the cheese will add more, especially pecorino. Last, cover the soup with the grated cheese and a couple of pinches of nutmeg. Replace the lid so the cheese softens, and in 2-3 minutes it's ready.

NOTE:
☐ Prized arborio rice imparts a distinctive creamy, yet slightly chewy texture to risotto and this soup, although brown or white long-grain rice can be substituted. Brown rice takes longer to cook, so allow at least 30 additional minutes of cooking time, or precook it according to package instructions.

5 PLANT-RICH

Robust in flavor and nutrition, these plant-based dishes include crispy Zucchini, Corn and Black Bean Fritters; also enchiladas, quiche, fried rice, polenta, nutrient-rich salads and a succulent take on a classic sauce for pasta, Vegetable Bolognese—a miracle of cauliflower, mushrooms, garlic and tomato. All are vegetarian, and most readily adapt to vegan preferences with the use of nondairy milk and cheese.

Creamy Polenta, page 58

Zucchini, Corn and Black Bean Fritters

Savory pancakes are a great way to enjoy a variety of vegetables in a satisfying, super-healthful meal. We started with squash, beans and corn, the revered "Three Sisters" of Iroquois tradition and added a Southwestern spin with black beans and cilantro. Sautéed onion contributes sweetness to the protein-filled beans and corn, and a deliciously creamy, fragrant cilantro dipping sauce turns this simple meal special. You can create fritters with almost any greens along with grated carrot, sweet potato, bell pepper...whatever strikes your fancy, is on sale or happens to be in the pantry. We like to serve these fritters as a main dish, ringed with sautéed zucchini or placed on a bed of greens. Fritters make an inviting appetizer and side dish, too, and can be prepared with various flours including spelt, rye, even a gluten-free combination of brown rice and buckwheat.

MAKES 4 SERVINGS | PREP TIME: 15 MINUTES | COOK TIME: 20 MINUTES | $1.21 / SERVING

1 small onion, finely chopped
3 tablespoons olive oil
2 zucchini
2 eggs, beaten
½ cup milk (or nondairy milk)
1 cup flour (wheat or gluten-free)
1 teaspoon baking powder
salt
1 cup corn kernels, cooked
1 15-ounce can black beans, drained and rinsed
* optional: 1-2 teaspoons cayenne pepper

FOR THE DIPPING SAUCE:

½ cup sour cream (yogurt is also good)
3 tablespoons fresh cilantro, finely chopped
½ lemon, juiced (about 2 tablespoons)
1 garlic clove, minced
salt and pepper
* optional: ½ teaspoon cumin

1. In a large frying pan, sauté the onion over medium-low heat in one tablespoon of oil until it begins to caramelize, about 7-8 minutes. While the onion cooks, grate 1 ½ cups of zucchini. Slice any remaining zucchini into ¼-inch-thick rounds.

2. Prepare the dipping sauce: in a small bowl, place the sour cream and stir in the cilantro, lemon juice, garlic, salt and pepper to taste and optional cumin. Return sauce to the fridge until ready to serve.

3. In a large mixing bowl, whisk together the beaten eggs, milk, flour, baking powder, 1 ¼ teaspoons salt, optional cayenne pepper and 1 tablespoon of oil. Add the cooked onions, raw grated zucchini, corn and black beans to the batter and mix gently.

4. Add the remaining tablespoon of oil to the frying pan and set it over medium heat. Once the oil shimmers, ladle about ¼ cup of batter into the pan to form each fritter (depending on the pan size, you may be able to cook three or four fritters at a time; just be sure they don't touch each other). Smaller fritters are easier to flip. Cook for about 3 minutes, until you see small bubbles form around the edges of each fritter and they begin to brown underneath. Flip with a spatula to cook the other side about 3 more minutes. They should be golden brown on both sides.

5. Transfer cooked fritters to an oven-safe plate or baking dish and keep them warm in a 200-degree oven while you finish making the remaining fritters. You may need to add more oil to the pan between batches. Any remaining zucchini can be sautéed in the same pan for about 3-4 minutes, or until attractively light brown. Serve the fritters warm, surrounded by sautéed zucchini, with chilled dipping sauce.

NOTES:

☐ These fritters freeze well in an airtight container and can be reheated quickly in a 350-degree oven—just until they regain their delightfully crisp edges.

☐ For gluten-free fritters, substitute ½ cup buckwheat flour and ½ cup brown rice flour for wheat flour. You will need to add two extra tablespoons of oil to this batter for moisture.

Veggie Fried Rice

Foodie fried rice is a good-for-you and tasty dish that can be as exotic or as basic as you like. We like to start with a base of white or brown rice and load it up with caramelized onion, crispy carrot, peas, a bit of garlic and ginger. Makes a quick lunch or dinner that pleases the whole family. So simple yet so good!

Makes 4 servings | Prep time: 10 minutes | Cook time: 30 minutes | 71 ¢ / serving

1 cup rice (white or brown)
¼ cup oil (a mildly flavored one like canola or safflower)
1 egg, beaten
1 onion, chopped
2 carrots, diced
¾ cup green peas (frozen)
¼ cup snow pea pods or corn
1 clove of garlic, peeled and minced
½ teaspoon ground ginger
¼ cup soy sauce
* optional: 2 tablespoons butter, 1 tablespoon each parsley and scallion, chopped

1. Steam rice for 10-15 minutes until cooked (30-40 minutes for brown rice).

2. Meanwhile, cook the beaten eggs in a teaspoon of oil in a medium-size frying pan, chop them up with a spatula or knife, and put them aside.

3. Sauté the onion in the remaining vegetable oil over medium heat until light golden brown, about 3-4 minutes. Add diced carrots and sauté until seared on the outside, but still crisp. Add frozen peas, snow peas and/or corn, rice, garlic, and ginger and saute a few more minutes.

4. Pour on soy sauce and stir the mixture until rice is coated with the sauce. Add the cooked egg and optional garnishes and serve hot.

NOTE:

☐ Fried rice is very versatile, as you can add a variety of veggies, depending on what you need to use up: green beans, bok choy, and broccoli are all good substitutes, and you can add cubed tofu, chicken, pork, beef, or shrimp if you're craving additional protein.

☐ Adding some butter at the end makes for an extra rich, flavorful rice. Stir it in while the rice is still hot so it melts.

EASY QUICHE

Quiche is a perfect and versatile meal in one dish. Easier to make than you might think, this French classic is amazingly economical. It takes just a few pantry staples and readily adapts to alternative ingredients. Broccoli and cheddar, baked together with eggs in a pastry crust, complement each other wonderfully. With onion, bell pepper, spinach, swiss or gruyere cheese, you can create your own combination. Appealing garnishes include fresh herbs or a dusting of paprika or black pepper. Serve the quiche warm or at room-temperature for breakfast, brunch, lunch or dinner along with a simple salad, and it makes pleasing picnic fare, too.

MAKES 6 SERVINGS | PREP TIME: 10 MINUTES | COOK TIME: 40 MINUTES (TOTAL ACTIVE TIME: 15 MINUTES) | 84 ¢ / SERVING

2 cups broccoli florets
6 eggs
½ cup milk (or nondairy milk)
salt and pepper
4 ounces cheddar cheese, grated (or nondairy cheese)
1 prepared pie crust (9-inch)
*optional: ⅛ teaspoon nutmeg; sprigs of dill, chive or other fresh herbs, minced; pinches of paprika

1. Preheat the oven to 375 degrees. To steam the broccoli: in a small saucepan, bring about ½ cup of water to a boil. Add the broccoli florets, partly cover the pan (covering fully will cause the broccoli to lose its bright color) and steam for 3-5 minutes, or until broccoli is tender and easily pierced with a fork. Remove from heat, drain well and set aside to cool slightly. (For other vegetables, see note below.)

2. Whisk together the eggs, milk, ½ teaspoon salt, pepper to taste and optional nutmeg in a large mixing bowl until well-blended. Then add the grated cheese and combine.

3. Place the pie crust in a pie pan on a baking sheet (to catch any spills). Add the broccoli (or other variations of your choice) and pour the egg mixture on top.

4. Bake about 35 minutes, or until the quiche is no longer runny in the center and the pie crust has turned golden brown. Remove quiche from the oven, let it cool and slice to serve. Sprinkle with optional pinches of minced fresh herbs, black pepper and paprika.

NOTES:

☐ Quiche will keep well in the refrigerator for several days. Cover with foil or transfer it to an airtight container. You can even freeze the quiche as the whole pie or individual slices; defrost in the microwave or a warm oven.

☐ You can make your own pie crust or purchase a prepared pie crust (from the freezer section of the grocery store). Prepared crusts save a lot of time and are usually not expensive, but see our Perfect Pie Crust (in the Key Recipes) if you're feeling inspired to make your own from scratch.

☐ If you're using chopped onions, bell peppers or spinach, lightly sauté them in a teaspoon of oil (in step 1) before preparing the quiche.

Quinoa & Lentil Salad with Lemon Vinaigrette

For a fresh take on salad, we like to combine lentils, quinoa, fresh herbs, raisins, feta cheese and cucumber with a creamy lemon vinaigrette. The key to great salad is that balance of textures and flavors—smooth, crunchy, sweet, tangy—and it's all here, complemented by a bright dressing you can make in minute. There is plenty of protein with the quinoa, lentils, cheese and seeds all contributing. Wonderful warm or at room temperature, this salad's flavors meld and develop when prepared ahead of time. At home or on a picnic, those around you will be enviously asking for the recipe.

Makes 5 servings | Prep time: 10 minutes | Cook time: 35 minutes | $1.53 / serving

1 cup lentils (preferably green, black or brown), rinsed and drained
½ cup quinoa, rinsed and drained
½ cucumber, chopped in bite-size pieces
6 ounces goat or feta cheese, crumbled
½ cup raisins
2 teaspoons fresh thyme, minced (or 1 teaspoon dried thyme)
1 tablespoon fresh oregano, minced (or 2 teaspoons dried oregano)
⅓ cup sunflower seeds (or other seeds of your choice)
* optional: 2 tablespoons fresh dill or mint, minced

FOR THE DRESSING:

    ¼ cup olive oil
    4 tablespoons lemon juice (about 1 lemon)
    1 tablespoon honey, agave nectar or maple syrup
    2 teaspoons dijon mustard

1. Bring the lentils to a boil in lightly salted water, lower the heat to a simmer, and cook the lentils, covered, for about 20-30 minutes according to package instructions. Note that cooking time will vary with the type of lentil. Most lentils are ready when they are just tender but still retain their shape. Remove from heat, drain and rinse with cold water to stop the cooking process.

2. While the lentils cook, bring the rinsed quinoa to a boil in 1 cup of lightly salted water, cover and lower the heat to a simmer. Cook the quinoa for about 10 minutes, until you notice a little white stem emerging from each grain and the quinoa is al dente, or tender to your liking. Remove from heat, drain and rinse with cold water to stop the cooking process. (When quinoa is overcooked, it becomes sticky and will not combine well into a salad.)

3. While the quinoa and lentils cook, prepare the salad dressing by combining the olive oil, lemon juice, honey and dijon mustard in a jar with a tight-fitting lid. Shake the dressing briskly for about 30 seconds until it becomes creamy and well blended.

4. In a large bowl, place the lentils, quinoa, cucumber and cheese, next adding the raisins, thyme, oregano and optional fresh dill or mint; last, add the dressing. Mix the salad gently with a spoon and fork until the ingredients are well combined. Taste for seasoning and add more salt if needed. The sunflower seeds can be added now, or if you prepare the salad in advance and prefer crunchy seeds, you can keep them in reserve until just before serving.

NOTES:

☐ Green, brown or black lentils are preferable for salad because they retain their shape when cooked—unlike red and yellow lentils, which are better for soups and stews.

☐ You can serve this as a main dish—it looks especially appealing on large leaves of romaine lettuce—or as a side.

☐ Don't have a cucumber? Try half a crisp apple.

Sweet Potato and Bean Enchiladas

These enchiladas are full of sweet, nutritious potato and onion, with black beans adding fiber, protein and another layer of taste and texture. Plus, enchiladas are not difficult to make. We're trying to eat more plant-based meals, and they fit the bill for satisfying, healthful and inexpensive. This recipe is versatile, too, as you can substitute other vegetables you have on hand. Bell pepper, zucchini, spinach, chard, corn, mushrooms and carrots are all good possibilities. Invite your friends or family to enjoy; if you are serving fewer, simply refrigerate or freeze any remaining portions in an airtight container and enjoy enchiladas without cooking on another day.

Makes 6 servings | Prep time: 15 minutes | Cook time: 1 hour (total active time: 45 minutes) | $1.33 / serving

1 sweet potato, cut in small cubes (with or without skin)
1 onion, diced
1 tablespoon oil
12 corn tortillas
1 15-ounce can black beans
8 ounces cheddar or jack cheese, shredded
20 ounces enchilada sauce
* optional garnishes: 1 diced avocado, sprigs of fresh cilantro, ⅓ cup sour cream

1. Preheat the oven to 350 degrees. Line a baking sheet with parchment paper or foil and place the chopped sweet potato and onion on it, lightly drizzling with oil. Roast in the oven for 20-30 minutes, or until softened and lightly browned. (If you are including spinach or another leafy green, lightly sauté it separately rather than roasting it in the oven with the sweet potato.) Remove vegetables from the oven and let them cool for a few minutes.

2. Meanwhile wrap the tortillas in foil and place them in the oven for the last 15 minutes of baking to warm them (warming the tortillas prevents them from breaking when you roll the enchiladas in the next step). Set aside 3 tablespoons of cheese for the topping.

3. Place a tortilla in a 9x12 baking pan and spoon onto it a small amount of the sweet potato and onion mixture (or greens, if using), black beans and cheese. Gently roll the tortilla, situating it so that the edges of the tortilla are held face down. If the tortillas start to tear when rolling, return them to the oven or heat each lightly in a skillet to warm them further. Continue filling and rolling up the tortillas. Arrange them tightly in the pan so they do not unroll.

4. Drench the rolled-up tortillas with enchilada sauce and remaining cheese. Cover with foil and bake for about 30-40 minutes until the sauce is bubbly, removing the foil for the last 5-10 minutes to lightly brown the top. Do not overcook or the tortillas will be dry.

5. Remove enchiladas from the oven and let them cool briefly before serving. Garnish each plate with optional avocado, cilantro or sour cream.

NOTE:
☐ Sprinkle any extra filling on top of the enchiladas or place in an airtight container and refrigerate or freeze it for another day. The cooked sweet potato and beans also make a handy base for tacos.

CREAMY POLENTA

Call it cornmeal or polenta, either yellow or white—it will do the job. After all, "available" and "economical" are our watchwords! Deliciously creamy, this impressive meal costs so little. Imagine climbing the stone steps to a tiny restaurant perched precipitously over Lake Lugano, encountering a giant fireplace and there, suspended on rusty chains over low embers, a massive black pot of...that's right, bubbling polenta. This recipe might just take you there.

Makes 4 servings | Prep time: 5 minutes | Cook time: 15 minutes | $1.58 / serving

        5 tablespoons olive oil
        2 ½ cups mushrooms, such as cremini or white button, sliced
        salt and pepper
        1 small onion, chopped
        1 pinch oregano
        3 ounces marsala (or white wine)
        3 cups vegetable broth
        1 cup polenta (or cornmeal)
        8 tablespoons parmesan cheese, grated (or nondairy cheese)

1. In a saucepan, set 4 cups of water to boil over medium heat.

2. Meanwhile place a skillet over medium heat, add 3 tablespoons oil. Add mushrooms with pinches of salt and pepper to the skillet and sauté mushrooms about 5 minutes, stirring or shaking occasionally to lightly brown them. Add onion and oregano and stir, cooking an additional 2 minutes to soften the onion.

3. Pour marsala into the skillet and bring to a simmer, then add broth and simmer another 2 minutes. Reduce heat and simmer gently for a few more minutes. Turn off heat and cover to keep warm.

4. Pour cornmeal slowly into the boiling water, add ¼ teaspoon salt and stir. Bring back the boil, reduce heat and cook for about 5 minutes, stirring occasionally. Stir in the remaining olive oil and half the parmesan. The cornmeal will be thick and the water absorbed. Taste for salt and doneness. If the cornmeal is still a little hard, cook a few minutes longer, adding more water if needed so the polenta is thick and creamy.

5. Serve right away, ladling cornmeal into 4 shallow bowls and spooning mushrooms and cooking liquid around each serving. Pass the remaining cheese at the table.

NOTES:
☐ If you don't have marsala, leftover white wine will still add fabulous flavor.
☐ Whatever Italian cheese you have on hand works: romano, asiago, parmesan, even provolone.

VEGETABLE BOLOGNESE SAUCE AND PASTA

Here, earthy mushrooms and cauliflower florets mingle their flavors and textures to create a whole new experience of Bolognese sauce. In the spirit of the rugged landscape where it originated, Bolognese sauce was built on meat, with a range of regional variations—so why not a vegetable variation? Not one that mimics a meat sauce, but one that celebrates the land's sustainable treasures? Marsala, ideally, or white wine if that's what you have, balances the tomato, and a generous addition of nutmeg adds another dimension. You control the simmer time according to your schedule.

4 tablespoons olive oil (preferably extra virgin)
4 ounces mushrooms (cremini, baby bella or white), quartered
2 cups cauliflower florets
1 onion, diced
3 garlic cloves, chopped
1 celery stalk, finely chopped
1 carrot, finely chopped
½ cup marsala (or white wine)
1 ½ cups canned tomatoes, chopped, with juices
salt and pepper
½ teaspoon nutmeg
1 teaspoon oregano
8 ounces pasta (your choice)
*optional garnish: 4 tablespoons parmesan cheese, grated

1. In a cast-iron or other deep skillet, heat 3 tablespoons of olive oil over medium heat. Sauté the mushrooms and cauliflower for about 3 minutes, stirring so they do not brown.

2. Add the remaining tablespoon of olive oil, the onion, garlic, celery and carrot. Stir, cover and cook the vegetables over medium-low heat to "sweat" them until they are tender and fragrant (but not browned), about 5 minutes. Stir once or twice.

3. Uncover the skillet and add the marsala (or other wine). Allow the wine to boil briefly, to release the alcohol, before adding the tomato, salt and pepper to taste, nutmeg and oregano. Keep the heat at a low simmer and cook, partly covered, for about 10 minutes.

4. Meanwhile bring a pot of salted water to a boil for the pasta, and cook the pasta until tender but al dente, according to package instructions.

5. As the pasta cooks, finish the sauce by placing it in a food processor or blender and pulse briefly—so it is still slightly chunky but also saucy. Return the sauce to the skillet, and if you have time, simmer it on low heat for a few more minutes. This is a good moment to sample the wine for dinner!

6. Last, add the cooked, drained pasta, turning and combining it well with the vegetable sauce. Divide the sauced pasta among 4 bowls. Sprinkle each serving with a tablespoon of the optional parmesan or pass the cheese at the table.

CHICKPEA-MINT SALAD

This light but filling salad is loaded with nourishment. Chickpeas are high in protein and fiber, while feta adds protein, calcium, B-vitamins and a foodie touch. The mint really makes it if you can find fresh mint reasonably priced (we grow our own, or rather it grows itself), though you can substitute other fresh or dried herbs that you have. Garlic crostini add a tasty crunch and are quick to prepare.

MAKES 2 SERVINGS | PREP TIME: 6 MINUTES | COOK TIME: 4 MINUTES (FOR THE CROSTINI) | $1.95 / SERVING

1 15-ounce can chickpeas, drained
1 tomato
6 lettuce leaves
2 sprigs fresh mint leaves, minced (or ½ teaspoon dried mint)
2 ounces feta cheese, crumbled
4 tablespoons olive oil
1 tablespoon balsamic vinegar
salt and pepper

FOR THE GARLIC-PARMESAN CROSTINI:

    2 garlic cloves, minced
    1 tablespoon parmesan cheese, grated
    2 slices of bread

1. Place the chickpeas in a medium bowl. Chop the tomato and lettuce into bite-sizes pieces and add them to chickpeas along with the mint and feta cheese.

2. In a cup mix together the oil, vinegar and salt and pepper to taste. Pour the dressing our over the salad, and with a spoon and fork toss until the salad is nicely coated.

3. For the garlic crostini: sprinkle the garlic and parmesan over two slices of bread and drizzle the remaining olive oil on top. Toast until the bread and garlic are lightly browned.

6 LATE NIGHT

Craving something completely delicious right now? Here are answers, with the cooking taking only as long as it takes to open and enjoy a glass of wine... or two. Turn flour tortillas into tantalizing Flatbread Pizza in minutes. For a hearty meal, toss vegetables and sausage onto a sheet pan with a splash of olive oil and let the oven do the rest. A quick, warm panini with brie and fresh pear does the trick for an easy gourmet sandwich. An excellent but so-easy Italian entree, Spaghetti alla Carbonara, is also a possibility when it is late and you're hungry—no elaborate ingredients needed.

Spaghetti alla Carbonara, page 72

FLATBREAD PIZZA NAPOLETANA

Our kitchen hackers discovered that a flour tortilla delivers the ideal consistency of a thin crust and can be loaded with sweet tomato sauce, veggies and a sprinkling of fresh goat or mozzarella cheese—for a real treat. It makes a quick dinner, late supper or tantalizing appetizer for friends. You can use cooked or uncooked flour tortillas; gluten-free tortillas are another option. Napoletana, by the way, is an uncomplicated sauce of tomatoes, olive oil, salt and oregano—a beautiful example of less is more.

Makes 4 servings | Prep time: 10 minutes | Cook time: 20 minutes | $1.09 / serving

1 tablespoon oil
4 flour tortillas (8-10 inch)
2 cups tomato sauce

TOPPINGS:

½ cup onions, thinly sliced
1 cup mushrooms, thinly sliced
2 ounces goat cheese, crumbled (or shredded mozzarella)

1. Preheat the oven to 450 degrees. Lightly oil a large baking pan or line it with parchment paper (so the flatbreads won't stick when baked), and place two tortillas on it. If you have two large baking sheets, you can cook four at a time, on upper and lower oven racks.

2. Spoon a few tablespoons of sauce onto the tortillas and spread the sauce evenly into a thin layer using the back of the spoon or a spatula, covering the entire tortilla (any areas that aren't covered with sauce will burn). The trick is to keep the layer of sauce as thin as possible. Scatter the sliced onions and mushrooms on top, and add the goat cheese (or mozzarella).

3. Now bake the flatbread in the oven for about 20 minutes, until the crust is crisp, the cheese has melted and the veggies are caramelized.

4. If a crisper crust is desired, transfer the flatbreads to a nonstick frying pan or skillet and cook over medium heat for 2-3 minutes more, until the crust turns golden brown on the bottom.

5. Cut the flatbreads into slices and serve hot.

NOTES:

☐ You can substitute other vegetables—like bell peppers, spinach, tomatoes, zucchini, artichoke and eggplant in any combination.

☐ Be sure to cut the veggies (except spinach) into thin slices so they will cook evenly.

☐ If you want fewer servings, keep the remainder of the prepared veggies in the refrigerator and the extra sauce in an airtight container in the refrigerator (or freezer) for more pizzas later. You can also make use of the extra sauce in another recipe, like Farmhouse Sausage and Vegetable Soup.

☐ For the tomato sauce, a jar sauce will do or you can make Classic Homemade Marinara Sauce (see Key Recipes).

☐ For an individual serving, you can bake the flatbread in the toaster oven.

SAUSAGE AND ROASTED VEGETABLES

Here's what to cook when you have assorted vegetables and not a lot of time to stand at the stove. It only takes a little chopping, and once the dish goes in the oven you're free until it's ready to eat. The bright vegetables sweeten with roasting and go nicely with chicken-apple sausage, or any other precooked sausage, and the caramelized onion. We like to keep things simple by seasoning just with salt, pepper and a good splash of olive oil—nothing else is needed. Plus, it meets all our criteria: simple to prepare, healthful, flavorsome and cheap.

MAKES 4 SERVINGS | PREP TIME: 7 MINUTES | COOK TIME: 30 MINUTES (TOTAL ACTIVE TIME: 10 MINUTES) | $1.66 / SERVING

4 precooked sausages (chicken-apple, spicy Italian, pork or vegetarian), sliced in ½-inch rounds
1 large onion, sliced
2 bell peppers, sliced
1 zucchini, sliced into ¾-inch rounds
1 large potato, diced
¼ cup olive oil
salt and pepper
*optional: 1 baguette

1. Preheat the oven to 450 degrees. On a large roasting pan or baking sheet, toss the sausage and vegetables with olive oil, salt and pepper. For better roasting, you want a pan that is large enough so the vegetables aren't crowded.

2. Roast the vegetables and sausage for about 30 minutes, until the vegetables are softened and the edges are nicely browned. Remove from the oven; add more salt and pepper to taste.

3. Place the optional baguette in the hot oven for about 2 minutes to warm it, and serve with sausage and vegetables. Dinner done!

NOTES:

☐ You can roast a variety of vegetables depending on what you have, what's in season and what's slightly past its prime in the fridge: eggplant, squash, mushrooms, carrots, parsnip, beets, broccoli and cauliflower all will be tasty.

☐ Softer vegetables, like zucchini, should be sliced thicker than vegetables that take longer to cook, like potatoes, onions and peppers. But don't slice any of the vegetables very thinly because they shrink in cooking as their water content evaporates, condensing their flavor.

☐ We like warmed, fresh bread alongside this main dish when we haven't included potatoes. The baguette adds about $1.29 to the total cost, about 32¢ per serving.

BRIE PANINI WITH FRESH PEAR

A luscious combination of creamiest cheese and slightly crisp pear slices, on bread, grilled in a pan makes a marvelous late bite. A red fruit jam, like strawberry or raspberry, adds a touch of sweet-tart that complements the rich notes in the brie. A fancy foodie treat, whenever you have it, at a great price.

MAKES 2 SERVINGS | PREP TIME 5 MINUTES | COOK TIME 7 MINUTES | $1.36 / SERVING

    4 ounces brie cheese, cut into ¼-inch-thick slices
    4 slices of bread
    1 pear (firm), thinly sliced and core removed
    2 teaspoons red fruit jam
    salt and pepper
    2 tablespoons oil (or butter)
    * optional: 2 teaspoons spicy mustard, like dijon

1. Place the brie, divided, on two slices of bread and layer the pear slices on top.

2. Spread the red-fruit jam over the pear slices and season with salt and pepper. Place two remaining slices of bread (smeared with the optional mustard) on top to close the sandwiches.

3. In a large frying pan, heat the oil (or butter) until it shimmers (or the butter gently bubbles), and place the sandwiches in the pan. Lower heat to medium and grill about 3-4 minutes, or until golden brown on one side. With a spatula, flip the sandwiches and grill another 2-3 minutes or until the cheese is slightly melted around the pear.

4. Remove panini from the pan and cut them into halves. Serve warm.

NOTE:
☐ If you don't have brie, the panini are tasty with cheddar, or try a combination of goat and blue cheese.

Spaghetti alla Carbonara

One of the best pasta dishes ever, this takes little time to prepare. How and where the sublime creation originated is not clear. Some insist that American soldiers brought eggs and bacon to Italy at the end of World War II and asked their Italian friends to make a dish with these ingredients. It has been a favorite of ours since student days, when carbonara was the only really good dinner we could afford to serve hungry friends. Now three generations enjoy it. Simple in concept, complex in flavor, carbonara tastes amazing—still.

Makes 4 servings | Prep time: 10 minutes | Cook time: 15 minutes | $1.54 / serving

8 strips bacon
6 tablespoons olive oil
pinches of red pepper flakes
8 ounces spaghetti (or other long pasta such as linguine or pappardelle)
1 cup green peas
4 eggs, beaten
8 tablespoons parmesan cheese, grated
salt and pepper

1. Cut the bacon into bite-size pieces and cook in a large sauté pan over medium heat until just done but not crisp. Drain off bacon fat (or don't, if you crave that richness). Turn heat to medium-low and add the olive oil (unless you're using the bacon fat) plus a pinch or two of red pepper flakes. Heat gently for 5 minutes, remove from the heat and cover.

2. Meanwhile boil salted water and cook the spaghetti (or other pasta) until tender but still al dente, according to package directions. Add peas for the last minute of cooking, then drain the pasta and peas. Return spaghetti and peas to the pot and stir in the beaten eggs* first, then the bacon-oil mixture. Add the cheese and toss to coat the pasta well. Taste for salt and pepper. Serve right away. *Be sure to add the beaten eggs, if not pasteurized, when the pasta is still very hot so that they cook through.*

NOTES:

☐ We use medium-size eggs in this recipe; for larger ones, decrease the quantity to 2-3 eggs.

☐ You can replace the eggs with ¾ cup of sour or heavy cream if you prefer. Take care to gently warm the cream with the cooked bacon (do not let it come to a simmer) to prevent curdling.

☐ While spaghetti is traditional, pappardelle and linguine are also excellent; a delicate pasta like angel hair or a robust one like rigatoni will be less so.

☐ In Italy, pancetta or guanciale is typical for carbonara; far more affordable in this country, bacon is our choice, and as foodies we let it infuse the oil for extra flavor.

7 COMFORT

Sometimes comfort means a cup of homemade soup. Other times it means roasted chicken or an indulgence like pasta melded with cheese in cream. There are so many recipes for mac and cheese, but this Creamy Mac and Cheese, a family specialty, is beyond creamy and rich with cheddar and parmesan. A treat for sure, as is the White Lasagne with Spinach, our update of a classic. For everyday comfort, we often turn to Pan-Fried Noodles with its array of vegetables, tofu and zesty sauce. Squash with Spiced Beef, a Native American tradition, works for weeknights and festive occasions alike. A truly Italian pizza (little work when you start with premade pizza dough) celebrates the seasons, and children adore it. For homemade Quick Chicken Soup, see the Key Recipes.

Creamy Mac and Cheese, page 88

Lemon and Garlic Roasted Chicken with Sweet Potatoes

Fragrant with lemon and garlic, this hearty dinner is surprisingly economical. A whole chicken is easy to prepare yet impressive on the table, and it makes 6 servings. If you have fewer for dinner, you can set aside some of the chicken for other meals and use the bones to make great-tasting chicken broth (see note below)—keys to saving you money and maximizing your ingredients.

MAKES 6 SERVINGS | PREP TIME: 15 MINUTES | COOK TIME: 1 HOUR (TOTAL ACTIVE TIME: 20 MINUTES) | $1.43 / SERVING

> 1 whole 5-pound chicken
> 1 lemon
> 6 garlic cloves
> salt and pepper
> 1 tablespoon oil
> 6 sweet potatoes
> *optional: cardamom-nutmeg butter, for the potatoes

1. Preheat the oven to 425 degrees. With paper towel, pat dry the chicken. Remove any extra parts (sometimes paper-wrapped) from inside the chicken and discard. Place the chicken breast-side up on a roasting pan.

2. Slice 6-8 small strips of yellow peel from half a lemon (the white pith is bitter), then cut slits in the flesh of the chicken and insert the garlic cloves and lemon strips. Save this lemon half (to squeeze over the chicken before serving). Slice the other lemon half into rounds and place them decoratively on top of the chicken; they will caramelize deliciously as the chicken roasts.

3. Season the chicken with salt and pepper and pour about ¼ cup water and ½ tablespoon of oil into the pan to prevent the juices from burning. Place chicken in the oven. Spooning the remaining oil (another half a tablespoon) over the chicken after 30 minutes will help it brown. Roast for about 1 hour, or until the chicken is golden brown and cutting into the thickest part yields juice that runs clear. You can also test the chicken with a meat thermometer, which should read at least 165 degrees at the thickest part when the chicken is done.

4. While the chicken roasts, pierce the skin of the sweet potatoes with a fork (to prevent potato explosion) and place them directly on the oven rack. Bake for about 40 minutes, until they feel soft to the touch or a fork can easily be inserted to the center of the potato.

5. To serve, cut sections of the chicken and place a serving with a caramelized lemon slice on each plate, spooning pan juices and the juice of the remaining half lemon over the servings. Cut open the potatoes, season with salt and pepper and serve them alongside. For the optional cardamom-nutmeg butter—our tribute to the great southern cook, Edna Lewis: melt 4 tablespoons butter together with good pinches of ground cardamom and nutmeg and drizzle over the potatoes. If you have fresh herbs or greens, you can garnish the plates with them.

NOTES:
- ☐ You can put any leftover chicken to delicious use in Lime-Coconut Green Curry and make Homemade Chicken Broth with the bones (see Key Recipes).
- ☐ To freeze cooked chicken for later, first remove meat from the bones and wrap it tightly; freeze bones separately.

Pan-Fried Noodles with Tofu and Soy Chili

This stir-fried pan noodle dish is popular with all ages—even our two-year-old can't get enough—and it makes a good, quick weeknight dinner. Onion, zucchini, bean sprouts and scallion went into the dish we made, though many other vegetables will do nicely. For example, broccoli, carrot, bell pepper, celery, spinach, cabbage, snow peas, bok choy and others that you may have in stock (avoid red beets). Chinese egg noodles, found at most supermarkets, can be replaced with rice noodles for a gluten-free or vegan variation. Be sure to boil the noodles until they are slightly underdone, because they will finish cooking in the skillet. A sweet and spicy soy-chili sauce, made in a moment, adds layers of flavor and leaves us asking for seconds.

12 ounces Chinese egg noodles
3 tablespoons oil (a mildly flavored one like canola or safflower)
12 ounces tofu (firm), cut into cubes
1 onion, chopped
1 large zucchini, chopped
2 garlic cloves, minced
10 scallions, sliced thinly
9 ounces mung bean sprouts

FOR THE SAUCE:
⅓ cup soy sauce (more or less, to taste)
1 tablespoon rice wine vinegar
1 tablespoon sugar (or honey)
1 tablespoon sriracha (hot chili sauce)
2 teaspoons sesame oil
½ teaspoon ginger (ground; or 1 teaspoon fresh ginger, minced)

1. Bring a large pot of water to a boil. Add the noodles and cook 2-3 minutes, until slightly underdone (take care not to overcook). Strain the noodles, rinse them with cold water and set aside.

2. Make the sauce now: mix the soy sauce, vinegar, sugar (or honey), sriracha, sesame oil and ginger in a bowl and set aside.

3. Heat 2 tablespoons of the oil in a wok or large frying pan over medium-high heat. Once the oil shimmers, add the tofu and cook about 5 minutes, stirring occasionally until it begins to lightly brown. Remove the tofu from the pan and set aside in a bowl.

4. Next, add the onion and zucchini to the pan and cook 3-4 minutes, stirring frequently; then add the garlic, scallion and bean sprouts and cook another minute.

5. Spoon the vegetables into the bowl with the tofu and set aside. Add another tablespoon of oil to the pan and carefully add the noodles (to prevent the oil from splattering). Stir for about 2-3 minutes, until the noodles are slightly brown and cooked through.

6. Toss the vegetables and tofu back in the pan with the noodles, stir in the sauce and it's ready to serve.

SQUASH WITH SPICED BEEF

Wonderful to make when winter squash is in season. Acorn squash, butternut, kabocha or even a sugar pumpkin doubles as the serving bowl, providing a presentation with flair. Ground beef and squash are spiced with an earthy mix of allspice, cinnamon, nutmeg, ginger and clove, with a little chili powder giving kick. There is lots of vitamin C and A in the squash and protein in the beef, so you won't go hungry after enjoying this hearty meal of Native American origins. Picture a pumpkin, stuffed with wild game and rice, baking in hot embers!

MAKES 2 SERVINGS | PREP TIME: 15 MINUTES | COOK TIME: 1 HOUR (TOTAL ACTIVE TIME: 25 MINUTES) | $1.91 / SERVING

1 acorn squash (or other winter squash), about 1 ¼ pounds
½ teaspoon cinnamon
¼ teaspoon ginger
salt and pepper
6 teaspoons oil (or butter)
2 teaspoons honey
½ cup rice
1 large onion, sliced ⅛-inch thick
½ pound ground beef
¼ teaspoon allspice
¼ teaspoon nutmeg
⅛ teaspoon clove (ground)
2 teaspoons chili powder
3 tablespoons ketchup

1. Preheat the oven to 425 degrees. Slice the squash in half to form two "bowls" and remove seeds. (See note below if you are cooking a pumpkin.) Place the squash, cut side up, on a sheet pan and sprinkle cinnamon, ginger and a pinch or two of salt evenly over both halves. Place two teaspoons of oil (or butter) and one teaspoon of honey in each squash shell. Bake for 45 minutes to 1 hour or until the squash is soft. Test by piercing it with a fork.

2. Meanwhile cook the rice following package directions. Sauté the onion in a medium-size frying pan in two teaspoons of oil until golden brown. Add the ground beef, allspice, nutmeg, clove, chili powder, ketchup and salt and pepper to taste; cook, stirring and breaking up chunks of beef until it is cooked through (no red or pink color remains). Remove from heat and stir the cooked rice into the spiced meat and onions. Taste for seasoning.

3. Remove cooked squash from the oven. Spoon the rice-beef mixture into the center of each squash bowl and serve.

NOTES:

☐ Cranberries are a pleasing addition to the meat and rice. Add ½ cup of berries for the last 5 minutes when cooking the beef.

☐ For a big wow factor, you can bake the spiced beef and rice in a pumpkin—but be sure it's a sugar pumpkin, not a jack-o-lantern pumpkin—or it won't be much of a treat and the trick will be on you! First, carve a lid and scrape out the seeds with a cooking spoon. Season the inside of the sugar pumpkin with cinnamon, ginger and salt (as above) before spooning in the cooked, spiced meat and rice. Replace the lid. Bake the pumpkin on a sheet pan, with ½ inch of water in the pan to prevent sticking, for about an hour, until the pumpkin can be easily pierced with a fork. Bring it to the table on a platter and cut into it with a sharp knife, serving some pumpkin along with the meat and rice onto each plate.

White Lasagne with Spinach

This unusual white lasagne has vibrant flavor and a delightfully silky texture. It takes a little more doing than most of our recipes, but is so worth it. In France and Spain, lasagne is often made with white bechamel sauce instead of tomato sauce. Combined with spinach and a balance of creamy and pungent cheeses, the bechamel gracefully binds the flavors and textures. In this contemporary version of the French classic, three cheeses—goat, blue and feta (or your own selection)—are melted into the sauce to evenly distribute the tang in every luscious bite. You can assemble this dish up to a day ahead, and with a quick bake in the oven, it's ready. Perfect for entertaining along with an antipasto, it is just as good the next day.

Makes 8 servings | Prep time: 35 minutes | Cook time: 30 minutes (total active time: 35 minutes) | $1.34 / serving

2 tablespoons olive oil
1 onion, finely chopped
1 garlic clove, minced
1 pound fresh spinach
1 ½ cups milk
10 ounces (total) feta, blue and goat cheese (or your own selection)
1 ¾ teaspoons cornstarch, dissolved in 3 ½ tablespoons of cold water
pinches of nutmeg
salt and pepper
1 pound no-boil lasagne noodles, (or regular lasagne noodles cooked according to package instructions)
½ cup of water
2 ounces Italian cheese (mozzarella, parmesan, pecorino or a blend), shredded

1. Preheat the oven to 300 degrees. Place the olive oil and chopped onion in a large pot with high sides over medium-low heat and sauté until the onion softens but isn't browned, about 5 minutes. (The high sides of the pot will make wilting the large volume of spinach easier.) Add the minced garlic and cook for one minute. Then add the spinach and turn it with tongs for about two minutes until it becomes brighter green, has softened and is reduced greatly in volume.

2. In a small saucepan bring the milk to a gentle simmer and add the feta, blue and goat cheeses (or your selection). Once the cheeses have melted, add the dissolved cornstarch and whisk until the sauce thickens slightly, to the texture of heavy cream. (If it becomes too thick, add a tablespoon at a time of water. If too thin, dissolve another teaspoon of cornstarch in another three tablespoons of water, and then whisk it into the bechamel.) Add two good pinches of nutmeg and salt and pepper to taste. Remove from the heat. Tip: go lightly on salt, as the cheeses will add some salt, too.

3. Spoon a layer of the bechamel sauce and three tablespoons of water into the bottom of an 8x8 baking dish or similar size oval dish. Cover the bottom completely with a layer of the lasagne noodles, overlapping the noodles slightly. Top the pasta with a thin layer of the spinach-onion mixture and another layer of bechamel. Repeat with another layer of lasagne noodles, spinach, bechamel and another three tablespoons of water. Continue to layer the pasta, spinach and bechamel until you use all the spinach and onion. The final, top layer should contain only lasagne noodles (you can double-layer noodles if you have extras), topped with a generous amount of sauce and a layer of the shredded Italian cheese blend. If you begin to run short of bechamel, you can add water to the mixture to extend it.

4. Drape a sheet of aluminum foil over the top of the baking dish and press the edges to the baking dish to lock in moisture. Bake until the sauce and cheese bubble gently around the edges and the pasta appears tender, about 30 minutes. You can remove the foil during the last five minutes of baking to lightly brown the top.

5. Allow the lasagne to cool slightly before slicing. Add a flourish of black pepper and enjoy. If serving individual plates, you can garnish with a spinach or basil leaf, cherry tomato or a sprinkling of chopped parsley.

NOTES:
- Cheeses: the bechamel sauce is just wonderful with a combination of 4 ounces feta, 4 ounces goat cheese and 2 ounces blue cheese, but use what's on hand—including fontina, Roquefort, an Italian cheese blend—and create your own combination. You probably know this, but we'll say it anyway: for this flavor profile (French, northern Italian), stay away from a Mexican or American cheese.

- Foil over the baking dish prevents the lasagne from drying out or browning excessively while baking. If the lasagne appears too moist at the end of the baking time, you can remove the foil and continue to bake it a little longer (it may be necessary to move it to a lower oven rack to avoid overbrowning the top).

- The entire dish or individual servings can be frozen in an air-tight container. Leftover cheeses can also be wrapped securely and frozen for later use.

Pizza di Quattro Stagione

A celebration of the four seasons and the time before pizza-with-everything existed. This ethereal deliciousness comes together in minutes with a little fresh tomato, a little cheese, seasonal toppings placed just so on the pizza and readymade dough. Our unforgettable first encounter with *quattro stagione* happened in Naples, where pizza originated. The pizza maker chose spring onion, artichokes, mushrooms and tiny clams, with each morsel in a quadrant of the pie. Do not pile them up! The trick with this all-but vanished tradition is a light hand, whatever four ingredients you choose. Olives, peppers, prosciutto, sausage, anchovy, fresh basil leaves and smoked oysters are all possibilities. Kids will delight in choosing and arranging their own toppings.

MAKES 4 SERVINGS | PREP TIME: 10 MINUTES | COOK TIME: 8-12 MINUTES | $1.61 / SERVING

1 pound pizza dough, at room temperature
2 medium tomatoes, very ripe, cored and diced (or 1 15-ounce can tomatoes, drained)
salt and pepper
pinches of oregano
1 tablespoon olive oil
4 ounces mozzarella cheese
1 scallion, sliced
2 marinated artichoke hearts, cut into quarters
2 mushrooms, thinly sliced
16 baby clams (fresh or canned and drained)
*optional: 4 fresh basil leaves for garnish

1. Heat the oven to 450 degrees.

2. Divide the dough into 4 pieces and shape them into balls. On a sheet pan, press out two of the largest, thinnest rounds you can make, leaving the edges a little thicker. (If the dough isn't "relaxed" enough to do this, press it out again just before adding toppings.) Repeat with the remaining dough on a second sheet pan, so that you have four rounds, each about 5 inches in diameter.

3. Place the tomatoes in a bowl and crush them with your hands or a fork. Season the tomatoes lightly with salt, pepper and oregano and stir in the olive oil. (For canned tomatoes, be sure to drain most, but not all, of their juices.) Thinly slice or shred the mozzarella.

4. Now spread the crushed tomatoes evenly over the pizzas and place the cheese on top (for authenticity, no cheese where the clams will go). Last, divide the toppings—scallion, artichokes, mushrooms and clams— among the four pizzas, with each topping in its own quadrant.

5. Bake pizzas 8-12 minutes, until the tomatoes and cheese bubble gently and the edges and bottom of the crusts are just tinged brown. Remove from the oven, decorate the hot pies with optional basil leaves and enjoy.

NOTES:

☐ Setting out the dough at warm room temperature for a couple of hours before you start makes it much easier to work with.

☐ Children will like rolling bits of dough into thin ropes to mark off the quadrants. Peas, bacon and sweet pepper are some child-friendly ideas, easily offered along with grownup toppings.

☐ Buffalo mozzarella is traditional on Neapolitan pizza, but cow's milk mozzarella is fine, too.

☐ If preferred, you can make two larger pizzas, each with the toppings.

☐ What to do with extra artichoke hearts? Add them to salad. Extra clams? Add them to our Classic Homemade Marinara Sauce for Spaghetti alle Vongole. For white clam sauce, just toss the clams in a pan along with their juices (or a good splash of white wine), some garlic, olive oil, salt and pepper and cook over high heat for a few minutes.

LATIN-STYLE BEANS AND RICE

Few comfort foods equal a simmering pot of fragrant Latin-style beans. Beans are prepared many ways in Latin America, and this recipe is a fusion of flavors from several cultures, making for a good-tasting but simple meal. Full of nutrients, beans are among the least expensive of all foods and they give you plenty of protein, fiber, iron and calcium. Preparing dried beans is much easier than you would think and doesn't require overnight soaking, though soaking at least 8 hours with baking soda greatly increases digestibility. The result is surprisingly creamy, tender, extra-flavorful beans, which you can serve so many different ways. You can use black or pinto beans in this recipe, and enjoy them over rice. Add a garnish or two—salsa, sour cream, grated cheese, chopped cilantro, sliced avocado, diced tomatoes, fresh chopped spinach or sautéed peppers and onion—or serve the beans wrapped up in warm tortillas. You can also enjoy them as a side dish. Save any leftover Latin-Style Beans for myriad recipes, as suggested below.

Makes 10 servings | Prep time: 5 minutes | Cook time: 2 hours (total active time: 15 minutes) | 37 ¢ / serving

1 pound raw black beans (about 2 cups)
8 cups water
1 onion, chopped
6 garlic cloves
salt
2 bay leaves
1 teaspoon cumin
1 tablespoon olive oil
1 lime, juiced
* optional: 1 tablespoon baking soda (for soaking beans)

For serving:

2 cups rice
* optional garnishes: sliced avocado, chopped tomatoes, chopped fresh cilantro, salsa, fresh spinach or other greens, chopped

1. Sort and rinse the beans to remove any debris. Soak the beans either overnight or quick-soak them if you're short on time. Soaking the beans is optional but makes them much easier to digest and reduces cooking time.
   Overnight: place the beans in a large pot with 1 tablespoon of baking soda and enough water to cover them by at least 2 inches and let stand overnight. Drain and rinse thoroughly. In warm weather, soak beans in the refrigerator.
   Quick-soak: place the beans with plenty of water and 1 tablespoon baking soda (as above) in a large pot and bring to a boil. Remove from heat, cover and let stand for an hour; then drain.

2. Place the soaked beans and about 8 cups of water in the pot. Add the onion, garlic, 1 teaspoon salt, bay leaves, cumin and olive oil. Bring to a boil, partially cover and reduce heat to simmer. Cook about 1 ½ to 2 hours, then test for doneness (depending on the type of beans, they may take more or less time). Add a little more water if you like more broth. If you prefer less, uncover the pot while the beans cook to reduce the liquid.

3. Meanwhile prepare the rice according to package directions. When the beans are done, squeeze the lime juice into the beans, stir and taste for seasoning, adding more salt if you like. Serve the beans over rice with optional toppings.

Notes:

☐ We used black beans for this recipe, but pinto and other types will also be delicious. You may have to adjust cooking time depending on the variety.

☐ Cooked beans will keep for 5-7 days in an airtight container in the refrigerator. Save them or use them right away in recipes you will find in this book: Zucchini, Corn and Black Bean Fritters; Cuban Picadillo; Easy Black Bean Posole; Sweet Potato and Bean Enchiladas.

CREAMY MAC AND CHEESE

We've spent years perfecting this family secret— it's so decadent that we only serve it to friends and family on very special occasions. The trick lies not only in the ingredients but how you combine them. We start with al dente macaroni, coated in butter to maintain a freshly cooked texture. This is key, because it prevents the sauce from being absorbed by the pasta. Then we fold in a cheese sauce absolutely loaded with the flavors of sharp cheddar and aged parmesan. Finally, to add a bit of crunch we layer cheddar goldfish crackers on top—guaranteed to bring smiles.

MAKES 8 SERVINGS | PREP TIME: 10 MINUTES | COOK TIME: 15 MINUTES | $1.66 / SERVING

1 pound pasta (macaroni, shells, wagon wheels or other sturdy, short pasta)
salt and pepper
¼ cup melted butter
3 cups heavy cream (24 ounces)
8 ounces cheddar cheese (preferably sharp), shredded
8 ounces parmesan cheese (preferably aged), shredded
¼ teaspoon nutmeg
1 cup crackers (preferably cheddar goldfish)

1. Bring a large pot of water to a boil. Add the macaroni or other pasta and good pinches of salt. Cook until tender but al dente, according to package directions.

2. Drain pasta and add the melted butter, stirring thoroughly. Do not omit this step or the pasta will absorb all the cheese sauce. Set the pasta aside.

3. Heat the heavy cream over low heat in the same large pot that you used to boil the pasta. Stir in the shredded cheeses, 2 teaspoons black pepper and the nutmeg, and continue stirring until the cheeses have completely melted. Keep the heat low or the cheese sauce could separate.

4. Remove sauce from the heat and stir in the pasta, coating it well.

5. To serve, top the pasta with crumbled cheddar goldfish crackers and some whole goldfish crackers.

8 WORLD FLAVORS

Spanish, Cuban, Italian and Vietnamese favorites, and more. Here is Andalusian Lentil Soup with the authentic fragrance and flavors of southern Spain—cinnamon, oregano, bay and garlic—perfect for a simple meal at home along with some cheese and crusty bread. Cuban Picadillo offers the distinctive interplay of sweet, sour and salty in a stew of ground meat with tomato, olives and raisins, and is usually served with rice and beans. The Vietnamese Salad with lime dressing is especially appealing as a main course in hot weather. And paella, the great glory of Spanish cuisine, is fabulous at any time of year. In Simple, Spicy Paella we share time- and cost-saving tricks so you can cook it and be feasting in an hour, whether you choose shrimp and chicken with the rice or make yours entirely with vegetables.

Cuban Picadillo, page 100

91

ANDALUSIAN LENTIL SOUP

This lentil soup is the best we've ever tasted— but don't take our word, give it a try! The character comes from North African spices that have influenced southern Spanish cuisine together with oregano, which grows wild on the dry hillsides around the city of Granada—where one of our team, Amanda, calls home. Leaves from the bay trees dotting the plazas of the Albayzín, Granada's historic quarter, also come into generous play. This vegan soup is a so-easy winter dish to prepare, though its full flavor will dazzle at any time of year. Lentils are incredibly economical and nutritious, rich in minerals, protein and fiber. Anyone looking to eat more plant-based meals need look no further... we're making this a regular in our dinner rotation.

Makes 5 servings | Prep time: 10 minutes | Cook time: 50 minutes (total active time: 30 minutes) | 71 ¢ / serving

¼ cup olive oil
1 onion, chopped
3 carrots, chopped
2 celery stalks, chopped
4 garlic cloves, minced
1 tablespoon turmeric
2 teaspoons paprika (or smoked paprika)
2 teaspoons cinnamon
1 cup lentils, rinsed
4 cups water
1 tablespoon oregano
4 bay leaves
 salt and pepper
pinch of red pepper flakes
*optional: 1 cup chopped fresh spinach, kale or other greens; a splash of lemon juice

1. Heat the olive oil in large pot over medium heat. Add the onion, carrot and celery and cook for about 5-7 minutes. Add the garlic, turmeric, paprika and cinnamon. Stir and cook for about 2 minutes more.

2. Add the lentils, water, oregano and bay leaves. Add 1 teaspoon salt, black pepper to taste and a pinch of red pepper flakes. Raise the heat to bring mixture to a boil, then partially cover the pot and reduce heat to a simmer. Cook for 35-40 minutes, or until the lentils are tender. (Note: cooking time will vary depending on the type of lentils used. See package directions.) If the soup seems too thick, add a little extra water and simmer another minute.

3. Add the optional chopped greens. Cook for 2 more minutes, or until the greens have softened.

4. Remove the pot from heat and serve. Garnish with an optional squeeze of fresh lemon juice and a sprinkle of paprika.

Notes:

☐ Soaking the lentils with baking soda before cooking the soup makes them more digestible by reducing or eliminating the phytic acid present in most legumes and grains. Place the lentils, 1 teaspoon of baking soda, and 2-4 cups of water (enough to cover the lentils) in a pot, cover and let stand for 6-8 hours or overnight. After soaking, drain and rinse the lentils in abundant cold water. This will also reduce cooking time to about 15-20 minutes (or less!) and require less water during cooking (cut water to 2-3 cups in step 2).

☐ An ancient source of nutrition, lentils vary in color from red, green, orange and yellow, to brown and black. We used green lentils for this dish; if you use another type, note that the cooking time may vary.

☐ Smoked paprika adds an interesting twist to the flavors of this stew, but lots of traditional paprika is also delicious.

GINGERY BEEF WITH BROCCOLI

Flavorsome, healthful, inexpensive, quick—that's a good stir-fry. In our recipe, zesty ginger sauce spikes broccoli and beef. Any number of other vegetables and meat, or tofu, combined with this sauce will make excellent eating and easy cooking, too. Think tofu with hoisin and cashews; fresh pineapple and pork; or mushrooms and spinach. At this cost per serving, help yourself to seconds.

MAKES 5 SERVINGS | PREP TIME: 20 MINUTES | COOK TIME: 20 MINUTES | $1.33 / SERVING

FOR THE SAUCE:

> 1 tablespoon fresh ginger, minced (about a 1-inch knob of ginger)
> 2 ounces sherry (or leftover wine)
> 3 tablespoons soy sauce
> 2 tablespoons sweet chili-garlic sauce
> pinch of sugar
> * optional: 1 teaspoon sriracha (hot chili sauce)

      3 tablespoons oil (canola or other mildly flavored oil)
      1 pound broccoli, cut in bite-size pieces
      ¾ pound beef chuck, top sirloin or flank steak, sliced across the grain in thin ribbons, about ⅛ inch x 2 inches
      ½ medium onion, sliced
      2 garlic cloves, sliced
      1 tablespoon cornstarch, stirred into 2 tablespoons water
      * optional: 2 sliced scallions; 1 ¼ cups rice, cooked according to package directions

1. Prepare the sauce by whisking together in a small bowl: ginger, sherry or wine, soy sauce, sweet chili-garlic sauce, sugar and optional sriracha sauce.

2. In a wok or large skillet, heat 1 tablespoon of oil until shimmering. Add broccoli and stir-fry for about 5 minutes, until browned at the edges, and remove to a bowl. Broccoli can be cooked in batches, if necessary, to avoid crowding the pan.

3. Add 1 more tablespoon of oil to the pan, wait a moment while it heats up to shimmering, and then add about half the beef and stir-fry for 5 minutes to produce a light brown sear. Remove cooked meat to the bowl with the broccoli and repeat with the remaining beef.

4. Add a little more oil to the skillet if it's dry, then add the onion and garlic. Stir-fry a minute or two to soften the onion.

5. Now add the sauce to the skillet and stir until it comes to a gentle simmer. Return beef and broccoli to the pan and give a few stirs to combine with the sauce. Add the dissolved cornstarch and stir to distribute it. Cook just until the sauce bubbles and turn off the heat. If the sauce seems too thick, stir in 1-2 tablespoons of water.

6. Serve alone or with jasmine or other rice. Sliced scallions make an appealing garnish. Pass sriracha sauce for extra heat.

Simple, Spicy Paella

At last, a paella recipe that is affordable and takes less than an hour to make! Paella, a celebration of rice, is the national dish of Spain, Valencia to be exact, where paella traditionally cooked over a wood fire made from orange tree branches. Our version uses shrimp, chorizo sausage and chicken, but paella is highly adaptable—variations abound, even variations made entirely with vegetables. Costly saffron is the traditional spice of choice, but we found that pimentón ahumado, smoked paprika, really provides authentic punch and the characteristic blush of the dish at a fraction of the cost. We even found a marvel of a substitute for the substitute! If you don't have smoked paprika, try sweet paprika with a teaspoon of cumin. In this recipe, if you wish for seafood to predominate, just go for it, and either way you will be off on a culinary experience that delivers you to another world.

Makes 5 servings | Prep time: 15 minutes | Cook time: 30 minutes | $2.53 / serving

For the marinade:
      1 tablespoon olive oil
      ½ teaspoon smoked paprika (or 1 tablespoon sweet paprika + 1 teaspoon cumin)
      1 teaspoon oregano
      salt and pepper

FOR THE PAELLA:

- 1 tablespoon olive oil
- 4 boneless, skinless chicken thighs, cut in 2-inch pieces
- 1 onion, chopped
- 1 red bell pepper, diced in ¾ inch pieces
- 2 precooked sausages (chorizo, chicken and apple, spicy Italian or pork), fully cooked, sliced crosswise in ½-inch disks
- 2 garlic cloves, minced
- ½ cup white wine
- 1 cup bomba rice (or other white, short-grain variety)
- 1 tablespoon smoked paprika (or 1 tablespoon sweet paprika + 1 teaspoon cumin)
- 2 teaspoons oregano
- salt and pepper
- ½ cup tomato sauce
- 1 cup water
- 6 ounces shrimp, peeled and deveined (about 10 shrimp)
- * optional garnishes: zest of 1 orange, sprigs of fresh parsley or cilantro

1. In a bowl large enough to hold the chicken, prepare the marinade by mixing together the olive oil, smoked paprika, oregano and salt and pepper to taste. Coat the chicken in the marinade and cover, returning the chicken to the refrigerator to marinate for 2 hours to overnight. (If you're short on time, you can coat the chicken in the marinade and go to step 2.)

2. Add a tablespoon of oil to a large skillet, braise pan or paella pan over medium heat. Dab the chicken with paper towel so it isn't wet. When the oil is hot, add the marinated chicken pieces carefully—to avoid splattering—and sauté for about 4-5 minutes, until the chicken has lightly browned.

3. Add the chopped onions, bell pepper, sausage and garlic to the pan and cook about 3 minutes, just to soften the onions. Slowly pour the wine into the pan, stir and allow the alcohol to cook off briefly.

4. With the pan still at medium heat, add the rice, paprika, oregano, salt and pepper, tomato sauce and water. Simmer gently, uncovered, for about 10 minutes, stirring occasionally.

5. Place the shrimp on top, cover the pan and continue to cook about 3 more minutes or until the rice is al dente and the shrimp is pink on both sides. Stir once or twice, if needed, to prevent the rice on the bottom of the pan from burning.

6. Check that the shrimp are cooked by cutting into the center of a shrimp; it should be white and opaque, not shiny or semitranslucent. Turn off the heat and serve the paella by spooning from the bottom of the pan. Optional: add a generous grating of orange zest to the top of each serving, along with a sprig of parsley or cilantro.

NOTES:

- ☐ Smoked paprika seems to be readily available these days in supermarkets. If you cannot find smoked paprika, regular sweet paprika with a few pinches of cumin will nicely suggest the smoky component.

- ☐ For a vegetarian version, omit the meat and seafood and add extra vegetables, such as sliced mushrooms and chopped zucchini, together with the onion and bell pepper in step 3. You can also add fresh or frozen peas or chopped asparagus for the last 5 minutes of cooking.

Vietnamese Sweet-Sour-Salty Noodle Salad

Zingy and bright, this refreshing main-course salad is fun to put together—a bowl of rice noodles topped with a variety of fresh, raw vegetables, some tofu or grilled meat and a lively lime sauce to drizzle over it all. We found cabbage, onion, edamame and pineapple on hand, and went with that. Almost any combination of 2 to 4 vegetables including cucumber, spinach, chard, carrot, lettuce, celery, bok choi, peas, bell pepper, corn, bean sprouts, scallions and broccoli, even a tropical fruit, will be delightful. To garnish, toss crushed peanuts and fresh mint over this sweet, sour and salty salad.

Makes 2 servings | Prep time: 15 minutes | Cook time: 10 minutes | $2.09 / serving

For the lime sauce:

2 limes, juiced
2 teaspoons sugar
2 teaspoons water
3 teaspoons fish sauce, or to taste (substitute: soy sauce)

¼ head of cabbage, finely sliced
½ cup onion, finely sliced
½ cup edamame (soybeans), shelled
½ cup pineapple, cut in small chunks
4 ounces tofu, chicken, pork or beef
1 tablespoon canola or other mildly flavored oil
2 tablespoons barbecue sauce (for meat or chicken)
4 ounces rice noodles (preferably vermicelli)
*Optional garnishes: 2 tablespoons crushed peanuts; sprigs of fresh mint, basil or cilantro

1. Prepare the lime sauce by stirring lime juice and sugar together until the sugar dissolves. Add the water and as much fish sauce as you like (it's strong tasting) or substitute soy sauce.

2. Prepare the vegetables by slicing leafy greens into strips and cutting other vegetables into bite-size pieces. Don't mix the vegetables together.

3. To prepare tofu, cut it into 1-inch cubes. Heat the oil in a skillet until it shimmers and lightly brown the tofu; remove it to a plate. If preparing meat or poultry, slice it thinly, then sear it in hot oil until it's cooked through, about 3-5 minutes. Stir in barbeque sauce for the last 1-2 minutes.

4. Cook the noodles carefully according to package directions—to avoid overcooking—and drain them. Place half in each bowl.

5. Arrange the vegetables on top of the noodles, garnish with optional crushed peanuts, fresh mint, basil or cilantro, and drizzle lime sauce over the salad. Eat with chopsticks!

NOTES:

□ Fish sauce, found in the Asian aisle of most supermarkets, is one of the defining flavors of this salad, but soy sauce can be substituted.

□ Pickled vegetables are often included in the salad mix and add excellent tang.

Cuban Picadillo

Picadillo is Cuban home cooking at its best. While picadillo appears in many variations across Latin America, we bow to a traditional rendition of this gratifying combination of beef or pork, green pepper, raisins, green olives and tomato. Typically black beans and white rice accompany picadillo for a delightful, easily prepared and budget-friendly dinner. Delightful, too, for entertaining.

Makes 6 servings | Prep time: 15 minutes | Cook time: 25 minutes | $1.47 / serving

3 tablespoons olive oil (or vegetable oil)
1 pound ground beef (or ground pork, or a combination)
salt and pepper
1 onion, chopped
1 green bell pepper, chopped
4 garlic cloves, minced
⅓ cup green olives (preferably pimento-stuffed)
⅓ cup raisins
1 15-ounce can diced tomatoes with their juices (or tomato sauce)
3 tablespoons vinegar + 1 tablespoon sugar, stirred together
¾ cup chicken broth (or vegetable broth)
2 bay leaves
2 teaspoons oregano
2 teaspoons cumin
¼ teaspoon cayenne pepper

    1 ½ cups white rice
    1 15-ounce can black beans, mostly drained
    *Optional garnishes: sprigs of fresh cilantro, hot sauce

1. In a large skillet, heat 1 tablespoon of oil over medium heat just until it shimmers. Add the ground meat, season with salt and pepper to taste, stirring and breaking up the meat with a fork. Cook to brown the meat on all sides. As it begins to brown, in about 3-4 minutes, add the onion, pepper, garlic, olives and raisins, stirring often. Continue cooking to soften the onion, about 5 minutes more.

2. Drain off any excess fat from the pan, then add: tomatoes, vinegar-sugar mixture, broth, bay leaves, oregano, cumin and cayenne. Stir to blend well. Adjust the heat to a slow simmer and cook, partially covered, for about 15 minutes. Taste for salt.

3. While the picadillo is finishing, set the rice to cook according to package instructions. In another saucepan over medium heat, place the black beans with a pinch of salt and heat through, about 5 minutes.

4. To serve, spoon picadillo onto each dinner plate beside a serving of rice and one of black beans, each in equal, wedge-like portions. Top with optional cilantro and pass the hot sauce.

9 BREAKFAST

Savory to sweet, quick workday ideas and leisurely weekend treats. Make a batch of your own Almond-Vanilla Granola and you'll always have a ready breakfast. The same goes for muffins, like the Blackerry-Lemon Muffins here, and both pair well with Coconut-Chia Pudding. When you make these breakfast staples yourself, they are not only more delicious but far healthier and more economical than commercial varieties. How about Quesadillas with Bacon and Scallion when it's time to kick back, or a Zucchini and Cheese Omelet with a side of potatoes? Sometimes nutritious Whole Wheat Pancakes with berries can be just the thing, or just a cup of good, strong coffee and a slice of deeply flavored Chocolate-Orange Banana Bread.

Blackberry-Lemon Muffins, page 111

ALMOND-VANILLA GRANOLA

Granola usually costs a mini-fortune. We can't figure out why since it's made of pretty basic ingredients. Plus, commercial granola often is loaded with sugar... too sweet for our delicate foodie palates! Try this healthful, homemade version instead. It's simple to put together and truly economical if you buy the ingredients in bulk. We use just a handful of costly almonds, adding flavor with vanilla and almond extracts along with a hint of cinnamon, and our taste buds dance. This recipe is a suggestion—you can combine pretty much any nuts or (less-expensive) seeds and dried fruit that you fancy. Maple syrup helps the granola clump, but honey is also good. You can substitute vegetable oil for the coconut oil. A batch of granola made ahead gives you a quick breakfast, and it can be stored for several weeks in an airtight container—perfect with yogurt, milk, our Coconut-Chia Pudding or by the handful for a snack. We've also been known to package up this granola in a mason jar, tie it with ribbon and *voilà*! A nice gift.

Makes 9 servings | Prep time: 10 minutes | Cook time: 1 hour (total active time: 15 minutes) | 83 ¢ / serving

3 cups whole rolled oats
½ cup flaxseed meal
½ cup sunflower seeds (or pumpkin seeds)
⅓ cup almonds, chopped
½ cup dried, sweetened cranberries
1 ½ teaspoons cinnamon
¼ teaspoon salt
2 teaspoons almond extract
2 teaspoons vanilla extract
½ cup coconut oil, melted
⅓ cup maple syrup (or honey)
¼ cup water

1. Preheat the oven to 275 degrees.

2. With a fork, combine rolled oats, flaxseed meal, sunflower seeds, almonds, cranberries, cinnamon and salt in a mixing bowl. Next add almond and vanilla extracts, coconut oil and maple syrup, or honey, and stir. As needed add up to ¼ cup water to help blend the mixture.

3. Spread the granola evenly on a baking sheet lined with parchment paper (for easier cleanup), and bake for about 1 hour, gently stirring once about halfway through. To help the granola form clusters, use a spatula to press the oats together after stirring.

4. Remove granola from the oven when it is just barely golden brown, as it will continue cooking briefly. Baking time will vary depending on the oven. Let the granola cool completely before transferring it to a container.

NOTE:
☐ For gluten-free granola, be sure that the oats are gluten-free, as not all are.

Zucchini and Cheese Omelet with Potatoes

For good reason the omelet is a French classic, and it makes our list for its versatility, tastiness and, of course, super low cost. You can replace the zucchini with whatever vegetable appeals to you, and choose the cheese you like. Grating zucchini gives it a fine texture that blends especially well with goat cheese, and sautéed potatoes round out the dish, guaranteed to leave you satisfied for hours. This is a favorite for Sunday mornings, and we love how inexpensive it is considering the result. This method, by the way, doesn't involve flipping the omelet out of the pan into midair—just fold it over easily with a spatula.

Makes 2 servings | Prep time: 5 minutes | Cook time: 20 minutes | $1.90 / serving

⅓ pound potatoes, thinly sliced (or whole, small fingerling potatoes)
2 tablespoons olive oil
salt and pepper, to taste
1 zucchini, grated lengthwise (or other vegetable, thinly sliced)
4 eggs
2 ounces goat cheese (or other cheese, shredded)
*optional: 2 tablespoons milk; 2 teaspoons fresh dill (or other herb), finely chopped for garnish

1. In a medium-size frying pan, sauté the potatoes in a tablespoon of olive oil over medium heat until golden brown and soft enough to pierce with a fork, about 10-15 minutes. Season with salt and pepper.

2. Meanwhile, in a separate frying pan, sauté the grated zucchini in about a teaspoon of olive oil over medium heat until just softened, approximately 2 minutes, and remove it to a plate.

3. Beat the eggs with salt and pepper to taste and (optional) milk until well mixed and large bubbles appear. With the frying pan over medium heat, add another teaspoon of oil and then half of the eggs, creating an even, thin layer; next, layer on half the zucchini. With a spatula gently lift the edges of the cooking omelet and tilt the pan to allow uncooked egg to flow underneath.

4. Crumble the goat cheese (or other cheese, shredded) on top just before the eggs are done, and with a spatula fold the edges of the omelet over, into thirds, and remove from heat.

5. Prepare the second omelet the same way, keeping the first one warm in a very low-heat oven. Season the omelets with additional salt and pepper to taste, top with the fresh herb, and serve the potatoes alongside.

NOTES:
☐ Whatever potatoes you have will be fine. Fingerlings are especially good with the omelet, but leftover baked potatoes can be sliced and quickly browned with excellent results, too.
☐ Other cheeses to substitute for goat cheese include swiss, cheddar, fontina, feta, parmesan and many others.

CHOCOLATE-ORANGE BANANA BREAD

It's hard to get enough of this banana bread. Chocolate and orange, from both juice and zest, enhance each other, and a dash of spice adds a foodie twist to traditional banana bread. It makes a luxurious breakfast if you're in the mood for a real treat, and you get to use up those very ripe bananas that are sitting around. Plus, the orange zest provides a colorful garnish. This bread keeps well and tastes even better the next day as it becomes more moist. We crave chocolate-orange bread for breakfast—and dessert—and often buy extra bananas just as an excuse to bake it.

3 ripe bananas, peeled and mashed
½ cup oil (canola or other mildly flavored oil), plus 1 tablespoon for pan
½ cup brown sugar
1 egg
1 teaspoon vanilla extract
zest and juice of 1 large orange (about 2 tablespoons zest and ¼ cup juice)
1 ¼ cups flour
⅓ cup cocoa powder
1 teaspoon baking soda
½ teaspoon baking powder
½ teaspoon salt
½ cup semisweet chocolate chips
*optional: 1 teaspoon allspice; pinches of confectioner's sugar for garnish

1. Preheat the oven to 350 degrees. Grease a loaf pan (about 4x8) and set it aside.

2. In a large mixing bowl, mash the bananas with a fork. Add the oil, brown sugar, egg, vanilla and orange juice and combine thoroughly. The mixture should look creamy.

3. In a separate bowl, whisk together the flour, cocoa powder, baking soda, baking powder, ½ teaspoon salt and optional allspice.

4. Add the dry ingredients slowly to the banana mixture and stir until well mixed. Stir in the chocolate chips and most of the orange zest, saving about a teaspoon to decorate the top of the banana bread after baking.

5. Pour the batter into the pan and bake for about 45 minutes, or until a toothpick inserted in the center of the loaf comes out clean. You can also press gently on the top of the loaf, and if it springs back it's done.

6. Let the bread cool, and sprinkle with confectioner's sugar (optional) and the remaining orange zest before cutting into slices.

NOTES:

☐ The allspice adds a subtle layer of flavor, but if you don't have any, don't worry—it's still delicious.

☐ To keep this bread fresh, after it has cooled wrap it in wax paper or cover with foil and leave at room temperature, or refrigerate. It will be even tastier the next day.

☐ You can store ripe bananas in the freezer to make this bread at a later date if your bananas are overripe. Just put them in with the peel on; then let them defrost at room temperature before cutting away the peel.

☐ Slices of this bread will keep in the freezer in an airtight container between sheets of wax paper. To reheat, remove a slice, and place it in the microwave or in a hot oven or toaster oven for a few minutes on an oven-safe plate.

COCONUT-CHIA PUDDING

Chia is a health craze that continues, and no wonder—it's a superfood. Chia seeds are one of the best plant-based sources of omega-3 fatty acids and also provide lots of calcium, fiber and iron. While chia pudding may be expensive at your local café, it's incredibly easy to make at home and only requires a few ingredients. Buy chia seeds in the bulk section at your grocery store for the best price or order online (about $4 a pound). Light, canned coconut milk, we discovered, provides the best texture and flavor—this pudding is super creamy. Add a little full-fat coconut milk for even richer pudding or substitute any coconut milk beverage. Blueberries and mint complement the coconut flavor, or top the pudding with fruit and nuts for a delectable, easy breakfast—or dessert. Try it, too, with our homemade granola.

MAKES 4 SERVINGS | PREP TIME: 5 MINUTES | REFRIGERATE: 2 HOURS TO OVERNIGHT | $1.04 / SERVING

⅓ cup chia seeds
1 13-ounce can light coconut milk
3 tablespoons maple syrup (or honey)
½ teaspoon vanilla extract
3 ounces blueberries
1 sprig fresh mint

1. In a bowl combine chia seeds with coconut milk, maple syrup (or honey) and vanilla; stir well.

2. Cover and refrigerate the pudding (which will look very thin at this point) for 2-4 hours or overnight. Top with berries and mint and enjoy.

NOTES:
☐ The coconut milk should be liquid (you may have to warm it gently) but not hot. If you like a thicker pudding, add more chia seeds; for a thinner consistency, stir in additional milk.

BLACKBERRY-LEMON MUFFINS

This homemade deliciousness is much better tasting, better for you and cheaper (less than 30¢ a muffin) than store-bought muffins. Enjoy fresh blackberries, raspberries or blueberries, depending on what's in season, or use frozen berries. These are a big hit with us for breakfast, and have been for generations — the recipe comes from our great-grandmother, who served them hot from the oven.

MAKES 12 SERVINGS | PREP TIME: 10 MINUTES | COOK TIME: 20 MINUTES | 27 ¢ / SERVING

2 cups flour
½ cup sugar
2 teaspoons baking powder
½ teaspoon salt
2 eggs
¼ cup oil (mildly flavored, like canola or safflower oil)
¾ cup milk
1 teaspoon vanilla extract
6 ounces blackberries (or other berries, fresh or frozen and well-drained)
* optional: zest of 1 lemon; pinches of cinnamon or confectioner's sugar for garnish

1. Preheat the oven to 400 degrees. Line a 12-cup muffin pan with baking cups or grease the pan thoroughly and set it aside.

2. In a large mixing bowl, combine flour, sugar, baking powder and ½ teaspoon salt.

3. In a separate bowl, whisk together eggs, oil, milk and vanilla. Add the zest of one lemon (the finely grated, thinnest, yellow part of the peel) for another layer of flavor.

4. Combine the wet and dry ingredients, mixing quickly and lightly with a fork. Add the berries last. Do not overmix or bother to remove lumps or the muffins will be tough.

5. Spoon batter into the muffin tin and bake for about 20 minutes, or until the muffins are light golden brown and a toothpick inserted into the center of a muffin comes out clean.

6. Sprinkle with cinnamon or confectioner's sugar (optional) and enjoy hot from the oven or at room temperature.

Whole Wheat Pancakes with Blueberries and Nutmeg

When it's time out for a relaxed breakfast, we think about pancakes—especially these big-flavored whole wheat pancakes with fresh berries, nutmeg and rich maple butter syrup to top it all off. Enjoy the pancakes on their own or with a side of bacon on a weekend morning. Set any extra pancakes aside for a quick weekday bite.

Makes 4 servings | Prep time: 10 minutes | Cook time: 30 minutes | 91 ¢ / serving

1 ½ cups whole wheat pastry flour (or white all-purpose flour, or a combination of the two)
2 tablespoons sugar (or honey)
1 tablespoon baking powder
½ teaspoon salt
½ teaspoon cinnamon
¼ teaspoon nutmeg
1 egg
1 ½ cups milk
6 tablespoons oil (or butter)
1 teaspoon vanilla extract
4 ounces fresh blueberries (about 1 cup)

For the maple butter:
¼ cup maple syrup, warmed
1 tablespoon butter, melted
* optional garnish: pinches of confectioner's sugar or cinnamon

112

1. In a large mixing bowl, combine the flour, sugar, baking powder, ½ teaspoon salt, cinnamon and nutmeg and mix well.

2. In a separate bowl, beat together the egg, milk, 4 tablespoons of oil (or melted butter) and vanilla.

3. Add the wet ingredients to the dry and stir with a fork or whisk until no lumps remain, but do not overmix the batter. Gently stir in ¾ cup of the blueberries, saving the rest to garnish the pancakes when serving.

4. In a griddle or large frying pan, heat ½ teaspoon of oil over medium heat until it shimmers. Using a ladle or a measuring cup, pour in about ¼ cup of the batter, depending on the size pancakes you desire. Once the pancake edges have started to cook and small bubbles appear all over the surface (about 3 minutes), carefully flip pancakes with a spatula and cook the other side for about 2-3 minutes more. Once they turn light golden brown on both sides, remove pancakes to a serving platter. Hold the pancakes in a 200 degree oven while you finish cooking the rest.

5. Continue cooking the pancakes, adding another half a teaspoon or less of oil to the pan between each batch. You may need to lower the heat slightly to keep them from burning.

6. Mix the maple syrup with the melted butter in a small bowl or jug to make the maple butter.

7. To serve, top pancakes with the remaining blueberries, drizzle with maple butter and sprinkle with optional confectioner's sugar or cinnamon.

NOTES:

☐ Try buckwheat flour, brown rice flour or a mixture of the two for a gluten-free version.

☐ You can make these pancakes with other fruits, such as blackberries, raspberries, cranberries, sliced bananas or small pieces of diced apple.

☐ To save time, we like to mix up a quantity of the dry ingredients and keep it on hand as our own premade pancake mix. Then all you have to do is add about 1 ⅔ cup of the dry mix to the wet ingredients when you want a batch.

☐ Pancakes can be kept in the refrigerator for a few days or frozen between sheets of wax paper in an airtight container to enjoy as a quick breakfast on weekdays—just bake in the toaster oven at 350 degrees for about 5 minutes until they are warmed through.

Quesadillas with Bacon and Scallion

Tasty and filling, quesadillas rely on tortillas to make the budget work. Incredibly easy to prepare, cheese quesadillas here become more interesting with the addition of crispy bacon and scallion, all topped with sour cream and fresh salsa for a foodie treat.

Makes 2 servings | Prep time: 5 minutes | Cook time: 15 minutes | 92 ¢ / serving

    2 strips bacon
    2 large tortillas (use corn tortillas for gluten-free)
    3 ounces cheddar cheese (or jack cheese), shredded
    2 teaspoons scallions, finely chopped
    2 teaspoons salsa
    2 teaspoons sour cream

1. Cook the bacon until crisp, pat it dry with paper towel and cut it into bite-size pieces.

2. In a large skillet over medium heat, place a tortilla and lay half of the cheese, bacon and scallions over half the tortilla (leaving the other half without toppings). Cook for 2 minutes, then fold the bare half over the fillings. Continue cooking until the tortilla turns golden brown and slightly crispy, flipping it once, at about 5 minutes. Repeat with the second tortilla, using the remaining cheese, bacon and scallion.

3. Serve with salsa and sour cream and garnish with any extra scallion.

NOTE:

☐ Did you know you can preserve any remaining cheese by freezing it away for another use?

10 SWEETS

For everyday and special occasions. Fruit crisps are always in season, and with much less sugar than most, the taste of the fruit in ours dominates. Enjoy the Apple-Berry Crisp for breakfast, as a snack or for dessert, and of course use whatever fruits you like. The two cakes include super-easy chocolate cake and an almond cake that takes a little more effort but can hold its own anywhere. The Rum-Chocolate Ricotta, which we've been making almost forever—since we first tasted it at a long-gone restaurant—is a silky, more healthful alternative to chocolate mousse that you can whip up in a few minutes with ricotta or farmer cheese. The coconut-orange pudding, Tembleque, is a holiday favorite in Puerto Rico. And the Truffles—what you don't eat yourself, you can give as a gift.

Almond Cake, page 125

TEMBLEQUE

A festive coconut pudding lusciously flavored with vanilla, orange and cinnamon, tembleque is a holiday favorite in Puerto Rico. Make it on the stovetop in minutes, and enjoy the cozy comfort of a pudding, with the wonderful flavor affinity of coconut and orange.

4 SERVINGS | PREP TIME: 5 MINUTES | COOK TIME: 15 MINUTES | REFRIGERATE: 2 HOURS TO OVERNIGHT | 76 ¢ / SERVING

> 1 13-ounce can coconut milk
> ¼ cup sugar, plus 2 teaspoons for garnish
> ¼ cup cornstarch
> pinch of salt
> zest of 1 orange
> 1 teaspoon vanilla extract
> ½ teaspoon cinnamon

1. In a medium-size saucepan, whisk together the coconut milk, ¼ cup sugar, cornstarch, salt, orange zest and vanilla.

2. Turn on the heat to medium and continue stirring as the pudding comes to a simmer and cooks. It will thicken in about 3-5 minutes.

3. Remove pudding from the heat and pour it into a serving bowl or individual dessert dishes. Once cooled, refrigerate for 2 hours to overnight.

4. To serve, mix together 2 teaspoons sugar with ½ teaspoon cinnamon and sprinkle it over the top of the pudding.

NOTES:

☐ You can replace the orange zest with tangerine, lime or lemon zest; or 1 teaspoon orange extract. Alternatively, increase the vanilla to 2 teaspoons.

☐ Regular or light coconut milk can be used.

APPLE-BERRY CRISP

Tart apples and colorful berries, cinnamon-scented and topped with hearty and healthful oats—it's one of the best breakfasts imaginable in cool weather. We crave it often. It's so easy to make variations on this family favorite, too, depending what's in season or on sale: apples, pears, peaches, plums, cherries, berries, and even pomegranate seeds can be used. A fruit crisp also makes a wonderful dessert—just top it with a scoop of vanilla ice cream or whipped cream.

MAKES 8 SERVINGS | PREP TIME: 15 MINUTES | COOK TIME: 40 MINUTES (TOTAL ACTIVE TIME: 20 MINUTES) | 74 ¢ / SERVING

FOR THE FILLING:

6 apples, peeled, cored and thinly sliced (about 6 cups)
1 cup berries (blueberries, raspberries or other berries)
* optional: ½ lemon, juiced

FOR THE TOPPING:

1 cup flour
1 cup whole rolled oats
⅓ cup brown sugar
1 teaspoon cinnamon
½ teaspoon nutmeg
pinch of salt
½ cup canola or other mildly flavored oil

1. Preheat the oven to 375 degrees. If you are using frozen berries, be sure they are defrosted and well drained.

2. Add the apples and berries to an 11x7 or 9x9 baking pan. Sprinkle with optional lemon juice and stir.

3. In a separate bowl, prepare the topping: combine the flour, oats, brown sugar, cinnamon, nutmeg and a pinch of salt. Stir. Then add the oil and mix well.

4. Spread the topping evenly over the apples and berries and bake about 40 minutes or until apples are soft and fully cooked and the topping turns light golden brown. Softer and riper fruits will cook more quickly.

5. Remove the fruit crisp from the oven and let it cool a few minutes. Serve it warm. So good!

NOTES:

☐ Granny Smith apples are excellent for a crisp, but any variety will do. If you are in a hurry or just prefer to, you can leave the skin on the apples.

☐ Brown and white sugar work equally well for the topping. Brown sugar gives a darker, more caramelized texture and taste. We go light on the sugar since that's what our taste buds prefer, but you can always sprinkle with additional sugar if you prefer a sweeter crisp.

☐ The crisp can be refrigerated and enjoyed for several days. Just store it in an airtight container and reheat in the microwave or toaster oven for a few minutes.

CHOCOLATE TRUFFLES

When only an indulgence will do... these truffles are remarkably simple to put together and require just 4 basic ingredients. Melt chocolate bars or chips, add a little cream and butter, and spice them up with vanilla, peppermint, or orange extracts. Roll them in cocoa powder or crushed nuts for an impressive handmade confection. We've made dark chocolate with peppermint and with salted almond, and variations abound. Truffles make a wonderful gift, but once you taste them you might end up keeping them all to yourself.

MAKES 8 SERVINGS | PREP TIME: ABOUT 5 MINUTES | COOK TIME: ABOUT 15 MINUTES + 1-2 HOURS REFRIGERATION | 81 ¢ / SERVING

> 8 ounces semisweet chocolate, chopped finely (or semisweet chips)
> 1 tablespoon butter
> ⅔ cup heavy cream
> ¾ teaspoon vanilla extract (or peppermint or orange)

FOR THE TOPPINGS
> ⅛ cup cocoa powder
> * optional variation: ¼ cup almonds, chopped and 1 teaspoon coarse sea salt

1. Place the chocolate and butter in a double boiler (a small bowl placed inside a small saucepan with a few inches of water in it) and heat over medium-high heat. When the water starts to boil, turn the heat down to medium. As the chocolate begins to melt, add the heavy cream. Gently stir with a spatula to see that it's evenly combined.

2. After the chocolate is melted and the butter and cream are mixed in, carefully remove from heat and add the vanilla or other flavored extract and stir.

3. Transfer the chocolate mixture to a shallow pan. An 8x8 baking dish or similar works nicely for this. Place in the refrigerator (uncovered) for about one to two hours, or until the chocolate has mostly hardened. (If you refrigerated for longer and the chocolate hardened too much, let it sit on the counter for a few minutes until it's thawed slightly and easier to work with.)

4. Line a tray with wax paper or set aside a large plate. Using a spoon or melon baller, scoop about two teaspoonfuls of chocolate and form into a ball. The chocolate will be quite sticky, so read our tips below for how to handle the chocolate. Roll the ball in a shallow dish of cocoa powder (or optional chopped nuts mixed with sea salt) and set onto the plate. Repeat until all the chocolate is used.

5. Serve at room temperature or chilled.

NOTES:

☐ This recipe makes about 16 truffles, depending on the size ball that you form. You can form these using your hands, if the melon baller or spoon doesn't work for you. You'll want to wear gloves or coat your fingers in cocoa powder, or wipe off your hands on a towel after each ball is formed.

☐ You can create variations using just about any flavored extracts or additions you can think of, and can top them with sprinkles or crushed candy for different effects and tastes. Salted almond topping pairs wonderfully with vanilla extract.

☐ If you prefer a less-sweet version, you can use 1 ounce of bittersweet chocolate with 7 ounces of semisweet chocolate.

☐ Keep truffles in an airtight container at room temperature for 2-3 days or store in the refrigerator for 5-7 days. You can also freeze these to enjoy later.

RUM-CHOCOLATE RICOTTA

Chocolate, honey and rum whipped together with ricotta cheese make for a wonderfully intense, silky-smooth dessert—like chocolate mousse only better, we think. It is far more healthful, too, and spectacularly simple to make. You can use farmer's cheese instead of ricotta. Serve it with whipped cream if you like.

MAKES 4 SERVINGS | PREP TIME: 10 MINUTES | REFRIGERATE: 20 MINUTES TO OVERNIGHT | $1.30 / SERVING

    8 ounces ricotta cheese (or farmer's cheese, 7.5-ounce package)
    4 teaspoons cocoa powder
    4 teaspoons honey
    2 tablespoons rum
    *optional garnishes: 4 tablespoons whipped cream, pinches of cocoa powder

1. Place all ingredients (except the garnishes) in a blender or food processor and blend. Scrape any lumpy ricotta down into the bowl and blend again, repeating until the mixture turns silken and glossy. If it's too thick to spoon out, add a teaspoon or two of water— or extra rum— and blend once more.

2. Spoon the ricotta into 4 small dessert dishes or espresso cups, chill 20 minutes to overnight (covered). To serve, add a spoonful of whipped cream and a dusting of cocoa powder. Done!

ALMOND CAKE

A fragrant confection inspired by artist Claude Monet's favorite, this not-too-sweet dessert is redolent of almond with a splash of liqueur adding an extra warm note. The cake keeps especially well and can be made a day or two in advance of serving. It's also versatile. Decked in confectioner's sugar and slivered almonds or fresh berries, you can serve it at a dinner party. This cake will also stand up to fanciful decoration by children.

MAKES 10 SERVINGS | PREP TIME: 30 MINUTES | COOK TIME: 40 MINUTES (TOTAL ACTIVE TIME: 40 MINUTES) | 84 ¢ / SERVING

> 1 cup confectioner's sugar
> ½ cup butter, softened, plus extra for the pan
> 5 eggs
> 2 tablespoons kirsch or other liqueur
> 2 ¼ cups almond flour (almond meal)
> ⅔ cup flour
> *optional garnishes: ¼ cup confectioner's sugar, sifted; ⅓ cup sliced almonds, lightly toasted; 8 ounces whipped cream; fresh berries

1. Preheat the oven to 350 degrees. Butter a pie plate or shallow 8-inch cake pan.

2. Cream together in a medium-size mixing bowl the sugar and butter, beating until smoothly textured and fluffed.

3. Crack eggs into a separate bowl, then beat them into the butter-sugar mixture along with the liqueur. Add the almond flour and mix well. Next add the all-purpose flour, mixing until it is well combined.

4. Pour the batter into the pan and bake in the bottom third of the oven for 30-40 minutes or until light golden in color.

5. Allow cake to cool before garnishing, if you choose, with sifted confectioner's sugar and sliced almonds or berries. With a sharp knife, cut the cake into 10 wedges and add a dab of whipped cream to each serving.

NOTE:
☐ Kirsch is flavored with cherry; other ideas are orange-flavored Triple Sec or brandy. Rum also complements almond.

Easy Chocolate Cake

Also called "Wacky Cake," this World War II-era confection was innovated from very basic ingredients—no butter, eggs or milk. Just toss everything in a bowl, give a good stir and bake. The result is a so-moist and chocolaty treat that can be assembled in a few minutes. Dusted with confectioner's sugar, this cake makes a gratifying dessert, and it goes well with afternoon tea. We enjoy topping it with a few berries in season. The cake never lasts more than a day at our house, but you can keep it tightly covered in the fridge for several days.

MAKES 8 SERVINGS | PREP TIME: 10 MINUTES | COOK TIME: 30 MINUTES (TOTAL ACTIVE TIME: 15 MINUTES) | 22 ¢ / SERVING

1 ¼ cups flour
¾ cup sugar
⅓ cup cocoa powder (unsweetened)
¾ teaspoon baking soda
½ teaspoon salt
1 cup water
⅓ cup oil (canola or other mildly flavored oil)
1 teaspoon apple cider vinegar (or white vinegar)
1 teaspoon vanilla extract
¼ cup semisweet chocolate chips
*optional: 3 tablespoons confectioner's sugar for garnish

1. Preheat the oven to 325 degrees. Whisk together the flour, sugar, cocoa powder, baking soda and salt in a large mixing bowl.

2. Add the water, oil, vinegar and vanilla extract. Stir to blend until the mixture is smooth and lump-free. Add the chocolate chips now and stir again to combine.

3. Pour into an 8x8 square or 9-inch round baking dish, and bake for about 30 minutes. The cake is done when a toothpick inserted in the center comes out clean, and the top center is springy when you gently press on it.

4. Remove cake from the oven, let it cool and dust with confectioner's sugar.

11 KEY RECIPES

Three cost-saving recipes that everyone should know. Better-tasting than store bought, they are easy to learn and you can put the results to so many uses. Homemade Marinara for pasta is a key recipe we wouldn't be without. Use it on pizza, as a sauce for pasta and as a soup base. For tasty Quick Chicken Broth, toss the bones from a chicken dinner into a pot to simmer for 30 minutes for a wonderful quick soup that's practically free. Perfect Pie Crust is another technique that's not hard to learn, and the healthfulness of ours, made with oil, plus its low cost, make it well worth doing when you're inclined to spend a little more time in the kitchen.

Quick Chicken Broth, page 132

Classic Homemade Marinara

Most everyone agrees that marinara has roots in Naples and that cooks prepared this simple sauce for mariners returning to port. So it's classic in one sense, but there are many personal and regional variations involving onions, parsley, carrots, chile peppers and more. At its simplest, and we think very best, it centers on tomatoes, olive oil and garlic, combined just so with a pinch of herb. The trick to "this really tastes Italian" flavor is the technique, which passed down to us from Z'Italia, our grandmother who reigned over a traditional kitchen in the hills above Naples.

Makes 7 servings | Prep time: 5 minutes | Cook time: 15 minutes | 43 ¢ / serving

3 tablespoons olive oil
2 garlic cloves (large), lightly smashed
1 28-ounce can whole tomatoes, preferably Italian and unsalted
salt and pepper
pinch of basil or oregano

1. Place the oil in a large saucepan and turn the heat to medium. When the oil begins to shimmer, add the garlic cloves, turn the heat immediately to medium low and stir for 2-3 minutes, until the cloves just begin to turn golden. Take care that they don't burn!

2. Now slowly add a large kitchen spoonful of tomatoes and their juice to the pan and cut and crush the tomato into the oil with the spoon. Cook for a minute before adding the remaining tomatoes and juice, crushing the tomatoes gently as you go. Next add ½ teaspoon salt, pepper to taste and a pinch of basil or oregano. Stir.

3. Bring the sauce to a slow bubble and partly cover the pan. Simmer for about 15 minutes. You can further crush the garlic cloves against the side of the pan if you wish. Give a final stir and season with additional salt and pepper to taste.

NOTES:

☐ Depending on the quality of your tomatoes, you may not need additional seasonings or herbs. We look for, and hope for, a dark red color. Taste to find out!

☐ If you prefer finer-textured garlic, mince it before cooking. For a smoother sauce, gently pulse the cooked marinara in a blender for a few seconds or use an immersion blender right in the pot.

☐ Use the marinara in many recipes, including Flatbread Pizza Napoletana and Farmhouse Sausage and Vegetable Soup (see index).

☐ For a quick bite, boil spaghetti and spoon marinara over it. Add canned clams, their juice and a pinch of red pepper to the sauce, heat and you've got Spaghetti alle Vongole.

Quick Chicken Broth

Homemade chicken broth is a tasty, efficient way to make use of the bones from a roasting chicken. It really enhances the flavor of soups and other recipes and contains far less salt than commercial chicken broth, all at a fraction of the cost. Keep the broth refrigerated for several days or frozen away for future use. If you don't want to make soup after roasting a chicken, just freeze the bones for later. If you don't have a roasting chicken, ask in the meat department at the market for a pound of chicken backs.

MAKES ABOUT 6 CUPS OF BROTH | PREP TIME: 5 MINUTES | COOK TIME: 30-50 MINUTES (TOTAL ACTIVE TIME: 10 MINUTES) | 12 ¢ / SERVING

bones from a whole roasting chicken (or 1 pound chicken backs)
1 onion, chopped
1 celery stalk, chopped
1 carrot, chopped
¾ teaspoon oregano
¾ teaspoon thyme
salt
7 cups water
*optional: 2 bay leaves, ½ teaspoon rosemary

1. In a medium-size soup pot, place the chicken bones (or backs), onion, celery, carrot, herbs, 1 tablespoon salt and about 7 cups of water, or enough to completely cover the bones.

2. Bring to a boil on high heat, then cover the pot and reduce heat to a low simmer. Cook for 30-50 minutes—even in half an hour you will get a nice, aromatic broth. Of course the longer you simmer it, the richer the taste.

3. Strain the broth into a large bowl and discard the bones. The final quantity will be about 6 cups of chicken broth. See note below for chilling the broth safely to refrigerate, if you aren't using it right away.

NOTES:

☐ To cool the broth safely, pour it from the cooking pot into two bowls; stir a couple of times as it cools. When it reaches room temperature, promptly refrigerate or freeze it in an airtight container: it will keep in the refrigerator for 3-4 days or frozen for several months.

☐ Use the broth in Farmhouse Sausage Vegetable Soup, Greens and Rice Soup, Lime-Coconut Curry (see index).

☐ For a quick bite, toss vegetables and noodles into the strained broth, simmer for 5-7 minutes and you have homemade Chicken Noodle Soup.

☐ For varied flavors, try simmering the broth with a teaspoon or two of minced ginger or with a few sliced mushrooms.

PERFECT PIE CRUST

We often buy prepared pie crust, but once in a while we like to roll up our sleeves and make our own. It's not difficult once you get the hang of the technique. While traditionally pastry crust is made with butter or vegetable shortening, we prefer oil because it's more cost-effective, less time-consuming to prepare, better for you, and we find the dough easier to work with. This recipe makes two 9-inch pie crusts that you can use to turn out a delectable variety of treats, from quiche to chicken potpie to good old-fashioned fruit pies.

MAKES 2 PIE CRUSTS (12 SERVINGS) | PREP TIME: 20 MINUTES | REFRIGERATE: 1 HOUR | 12 ¢ / SERVING

> 3 cups flour
> 1 teaspoon salt
> 1 teaspoon sugar (for sweet pies)
> 1 cup canola, safflower or other mildly flavored oil
> 6 tablespoons water (ice cold)

1. In a large mixing bowl, stir together the flour, 1 teaspoon salt (and optional sugar for a sweet pie).

2. Add oil and ice water to the flour. With your hands or a wooden spoon, blend the ingredients. Add a little more flour if the dough is too moist. If it's too dry, add a few more drops of ice water to hold the dough together. It should be a bit crumbly but not sticky.

3. On a floured surface, knead the dough a couple of times until it is a uniform, smooth texture. Divide the dough in half and form 2 balls. Cover each one in plastic wrap or wax paper and refrigerate for at least an hour. Chilling the dough makes it easier to roll out in the next step.

4. On a floured surface, roll out a ball of dough until it is about ⅛-inch thick. You can also roll it between two pieces of plastic wrap or wax paper to prevent sticking. If you don't have a rolling pin, use a wine bottle.

5. Press the dough into a pie dish, and you're all set to prepare your favorite quiche or pie! Repeat the process for the second pie crust, or save it for another time.

NOTES:

☐ You can partially bake the pie crust before adding the ingredients for a quiche or pie if you like a crisper crust, but it's not necessary. To partially bake the crust, prick a few holes in the bottom with a fork (to prevent it from bubbling up during baking) and bake at 400 degrees for 7-9 minutes. Remove from the oven and let it cool before continuing with your recipe.

☐ You can refrigerate dough for a few days after step 3 until you are ready to use it. Just keep it covered in wax paper or plastic wrap for up to 5 days. You can also freeze the dough in an airtight container for later use. Place frozen dough in the refrigerator to thaw overnight.

☐ This recipe calls for oil, but you can substitute butter if you prefer. Add a cup of chilled unsalted butter, cut into ½-inch cubes, to the flour and salt, and with your fingertips rub the butter into the flour to make very small crumbles. Then add the ice water and blend the dough quickly.

☐ Use the pie crust to make Easy Quiche (page 52) and Chicken, Herb, and Sweet Corn Pie (thefivedollarfoodie.com).

☐ For apple pie, peel, core and slice 6-8 apples, toss them with 2 teaspoons of cinnamon and place in the pie crust. Sprinkle a tablespoon of sugar over the top. Bake at 375 degrees for about 45 minutes, until the apples are soft.

INDEX

PUDDING
Coconut-Chia Pudding **110**
Rum-Chocolate Ricotta **124**
Tembleque **118**

SALADS
Chickpea-Mint **62**
Quinoa and Lentil **54**
Vietnamese Sweet-Sour-Salty Noodle **98**

SANDWICHES
Brie Panini with Fresh Pear **70**
Olive and Herb Tuna Wrap **20**

SEAFOOD
Marinara Sauce with Clams **130**
   (see Classic Homemade Marinara, notes)
Olive and Herb Tuna Wrap **20**
Simple, Spicy Paella **96**

SOUP
Andalusian Lentil **92**
Classic Onion **40**
Farmhouse Sausage and Vegetable **36**
Greens and Rice **44**
Velvet Corn Chowder **42**
White Bean **18**

VEGAN *&* VEGETARIAN*
Almond Cake* **125**
Almond-Vanilla Granola **104**
Andalusian Lentil Soup **92**
Apple-Berry Crisp **120**
Apple Pie **133**
   (see Perfect Pie Crust, notes)
Blackberry-Lemon Muffins* **111**
Brie Panini with Fresh Pear* **70**

Chickpea-Mint Salad* **62**
Classic Homemade Marinara Sauce **130**
Coconut-Chia Pudding **110**
Creamy Mac and Cheese* **88**
Creamy Polenta **58**
Easy Black Bean Posole **26**
Easy Chocolate Cake **126**
Easy Quiche* **52**
Flatbread Pizza Napoletana* **66**
Ginger Curried Lentils **22**
Latin-Style Beans and Rice **86**
Pan-Fried Noodles with Tofu and Soy Chili* **78**
Potatoes Gratin with Glazed Carrots* **24**
Quinoa and Lentil Salad* **54**
Rum-Chocolate Ricotta* **124**
Spaghetti Aglio e Olio **28**
Sweet Potato and Bean Enchiladas* **56**
Sweet Potato Chili* **34**
   (see Chili with Cinnamon and Cacao, notes)
Tembleque **118**
Vegetable Bolognese Sauce and Pasta **60**
Veggie Fried Rice **50**
Velvet Corn Chowder **42**
Vietnamese Sweet-Sour-Salty Noodle Salad **98**
White Bean Soup **18**
White Lasagne with Spinach* **82**
Zucchini, Corn and Black Bean Fritters* **48**

*Starred recipes are vegetarian and contain dairy ingredients. For vegan preferences, replace with plant-based cheese, yogurt, milk or egg substitute.

CPSIA information can be obtained
at www.ICGtesting.com
Printed in the USA
LVHW070224271121
704418LV00016B/68